THE PLAYS OF EMILE VERHAEREN

THE PLAYS OF EMILE
VERHAEREN

THE DAWN: THE CLOISTER:
PHILIP II: HELEN
OF SPARTA

WILDSIDE PRESS

CONTENTS

THE DAWN

A PLAY IN FOUR ACTS

TRANSLATED BY

ARTHUR SYMONS

B-

NOTE

LES AUBES was first published in 1898 by Ed. Deman, Brussels. The English version, by Mr. Arthur Symons, now republished, appeared later in the same year (London, Duckworth and Co.). The play was privately produced by the Section d'Art de la Maison du Peuple de Bruxelles before its appearance in book form. It has not yet been publicly performed.

In his introduction to the first edition of his translation Mr. Symons wrote: "I have translated M. Verhaeren's verse very literally, and I have followed all his rhythms with great exactitude. But for the most part I have used unrhymed in place of rhymed verse, reserving rhyme for the speeches of the Seer, which are in a more definitely stanzaic form in the original, and for the *ronde* on page 90. It seemed to me this was the best way of conveying M. Verhaeren's form into English; and, having finished my translation, I wrote to him, telling him exactly what I had done. He replied: 'Si le vers français sans rime existait, je l'aurais employé moi-même. Seulement le vers blanc français ne me dit rien. En anglais ce doit être mon souhait. Je vous approuve donc entièrement.'"

PERSONS OF THE DRAMA

THE CROWD.

GROUPS: WORKMEN, BEGGARS, FARMERS, SOLDIERS, WOMEN, YOUNG MEN AND WOMEN, PASSERS, BOYS, OLD MEN.

JACQUES HÉRÉNIEN, *tribune*.

PIERRE HÉRÉNIEN, *his father*.

CLAIRE, *his wife*.

GEORGES, *his son*.

HAINEAU, *brother of* CLAIRE.

HORDAIN, *captain of the enemy, disciple of* HÉRÉNIEN.

OLD GHISLAIN, *farmer*.

THE CURÉ.

AN OFFICER.

AN EMISSARY.

A GIPSY.

A CONSUL *of Oppidomagne*.

THE SHEPHERD.

THE BEGGAR BENOIT.

THE SEER *of the Villages*.

THE SEER *of the Cities*.

The groups act as a single person of multiple and contradictory aspects.

5

THE DAWN

ACT I

SCENE I

*An immense open space into which converge, on the right,
the roads descending from Oppidomagne ; on the
left, the paths rising from the plains. Lines of
trees accompany them as far as the eye can see.
The enemy has surrounded the town. The country
is on fire. Great flaring lights in the distance;
the tocsin sounds.*

*Groups of beggars fill the trenches. Others, standing
on gravel-heaps, scan the distance, and cry to one
another.*

THE BEGGARS.
LOOK, from this mound you can see the villages
all on fire.

—Climb the trees: we can see better.

[*A beggar, clinging to a tree.*

—This way ! this way !

BEGGARS. [*Looking towards the town.*]

—The flames are getting brighter and bigger, towards the town.

—The powder-mills are blowing up.

[*The sound of firing and explosions.*

The works at the port are on fire, and the quays,

7

and the docks. The petroleum-sheds have caught fire. Yards and masts burn black, and make crosses against the sky!

BEGGARS. [*Looking towards the plains.*]
—The country is all red, over the plains. The fire has got hold of Hérénien's farm: they are throwing the furniture into the street, pell mell. They are bringing the beasts out of the stable with covered heads. They are carrying out the old sick father on his great bed.

—It is the farmer's turn now to have death on his heels.

—Ah! what a fine, quick vengeance! They are cast out themselves, they who cast us out. The crowd of them heaps the highways. All our curses have carried; all our blasphemies, all our prayers, all our angers!

—See there, the cattle flying to the fens,
The stallions rear and snap the trace in two,
And snort against this woeful torch;
And one has fled, with burning at his heels
And death upon his flying mane,
He turns his head about, and bites the flame
That eats upon his neck;
Look all of you, and see the hands
Of madmen piling up the flame with pitchforks.

—The bells madden in the wind. Churches and towers crumble. God Himself might have fear.

—Who knows why this war was unchained?

—All the kings desire Oppidomagne. They desire it to the ends of the earth.

[*People rush up excitedly, and disappear confusedly in every direction. Some stop, and cry:*

—The farmers are piling up their furniture and

8

THE DAWN

their clothes on waggons; they are coming towards
the town; they will pass here.

THE GROUP OF BEGGARS.
—This is the moment to make for Oppidomagne.
—Follow them.

THE BEGGAR BENOIT.
Follow them? And of what race are *you*, then?
Since you and I have been revolters, vagabonds,
Yes, you and I, all of us, all the time,
Have not these farming, homestead folk
Bent us and broken us with aching poverty?
They, they have been the bread,
And we, we have so sorely been the hunger,
That the sharp flames which eat
Their bursting granaries now
Seem to me like our very teeth
And the malevolent tearing of our vehement nails!
Since I have come and gone, and come and gone,
        and come again,
Barring with evil luck
The gates at which I beg,
My hands have spread the sickness that they breed,
My hands have rooted up their dead,
Have stolen their dead, my aged hands
Have gagged their daughters, and have ravished them;
I hate them as a man may hate
The evillest thing upon the earth;
And now at least let them be bashed
With their own pikes and their own poles.

AN OLD MAN.
What is the good of bashing them? They will do
no more harm; they are more wretched than we are.

9

THE DAWN

THE BEGGAR BENOIT.
Be silent, you are too old to be a man any longer.
[*Fresh bands hurry along the Oppidomagne
road. A group of workmen appears.
One of them speaks to the beggars.*

THE WORKMAN.
Has Hérénien passed yet?

A BEGGAR. [*To the workman.*]
The shepherd knows him. Ask him.

THE WORKMAN. [*To the shepherd.*]
Has Hérénien passed here?

THE SHEPHERD. [*In rags.*]
I am waiting for him. He has gone to look after
his father. I want to see him again. I cured him
when he was a child.

THE WORKMAN.
He is sure to come. We will wait for him together.

THE SHEPHERD.
How has he left the city? His enemies themselves
ought to have kept him there.

THE WORKMAN.
Hérénien does what he likes. His father was dying
at the village, and called him.

THE SHEPHERD.
Do you think he will conquer Oppidomagne?

THE WORKMAN.
Is he not the master of the people?
He is that wonderful and sacred thing

THE DAWN

That lives, beyond the shadow of this hour,
Already in the future, which he touches;
None better have discerned than he
How much of folly mixed with how much wisdom
    waits
To bring the new to-morrows in;
His clear books cast a light on all we think about.
'Tis there we other mortals learn
What is the way that leads to good
And what exalts a man, at such an hour, to be a
    God.

THE SHEPHERD.
You are one of those who love and defend him in
the city.

THE WORKMAN.
Hundreds we are, thousands we are
Who worship him, and follow him,
No matter where he goes, unto the very end.

> [*The workman goes on ahead, to watch for*
> HÉRÉNIEN. *More people in flight,*
> *then a group of peasants dragging after*
> *them carts and hand-carts. The horses*
> *have climbed the hill, with heavy loads.*

OLD GHISLAIN.
Our beasts are tired out. Let them get wind again.
Hallo, there, you beggars, has that scoundrel Hérénien
passed this way?

THE BEGGAR BENOIT.
Old Ghislain, be silent.

OLD GHISLAIN.
Be silent! be silent! why? who for? Hérénien is
one of you then?

11

THE DAWN

THE BEGGAR BENOIT.

Old Ghislain, we are the power here, and we can strike you down, before you have so much time as to cry murder. If, for all these years and these years, you have thrown to us at your doors the refuse of your pigs and the washings of your kitchen, we too, for all these years and these years, have we not given you our prayers and our *aves?* We are quits for the past, and the present is ours.

> [*He advances towards* FATHER GHISLAIN *menacingly.*]

A PEASANT. [*Running up.*]

Old Ghislain, Old Ghislain, your farm, "Tinkling Meadow," has spread the fire to the whole of "Wolf Plain."
The trees are burning, on the roads,
And the whole fir-wood snorts
And cries and howls aloud,
And all the flames spire up,
Up to the clouds,
And the flames bite the very sky!

OLD GHISLAIN.

Well, and what then? and what has that to do with
    me?
Let all the plain and all the woods begone,
And let the wind, the air, and the sky burn,
And let the earth itself break as a pebble breaks.

> [*With a change of tone.*]

Just now this beggar talked of killing me.

> [*To the beggar* BENOIT.]

Well, do it, then; be quick with you!
Here are my hands, here are my arms, that I have
    sold
For a vain labour; here too is my obstinate brain;

12

THE DAWN

Here is my skin withered in all its pores,
Here is my back, here are the rags of me,
The ruin that I drag about
All the long years, all the long years!
Truly I ask myself, why is it that I live?
I dig a field the frost will reap,
I farm the meadows that are evil-starred;
All that my father hoarded up, farthing by farthing,
    all
That he had squeezed, and hid, and burrowed, like
    a miser,
I have lost all, eaten it all.
I have implored my sons: they have devoured me;
They have been swallowed up in the unfruitful town,
They have preferred a life unfruitful, infamous;
Hamlets and little towns are dead;
Oppidomagne has sapped the strength of them,
Oppidomagne has drained the blood of them;
And now, behold
In every acre and in every close
Branching abroad the several maladies
Of water and of earth and air and sun!

A PEASANT.
Your sorrows are ours. We are all equally wretched.

OLD GHISLAIN.
When I was but a child, we feasted sowing-time,
The soil was kindly then to folk and to horned
    beasts,
The flax came up like happiness in flower.
But now, but now men fear the earth.
And surely needs must something have been violated,
Some sacred and some obscure thing;
Now 'tis the coal that all belongs to, kept,
Once, in the covering night.

13

THE DAWN

The netted rails, upon the plains bestarred
With golden signals, swarm;
Trains graze the meadow-lands, and pierce the banks;
The living skies are eaten up with piercing smoke;
The grass bleeds, and the virgin herb, harvest itself,
Feed on the sulphur's poisonous breath.
'Tis now
That, terrible in victory, come forth
Iron, and lead, and fire;
And hell itself comes forth with them!
　　　　[*The beggars recoil, and cease to threaten.*

A BEGGAR.
Poor man!

OLD GHISLAIN.
Poor man! But no! [*Drawing towards him a peasant,
and pointing to an enclosure which is burning.*] You
think, do you, that it was the enemy set fire to
my enclosure? Undeceive yourselves. [*Showing his
hands.*] It was these two hands.
And my woods by "Firefly Pond"? These hands
again. And my granaries and my ricks? These
always. No, no, Old Ghislain isn't a poor man. It
is he, he only perhaps, who sees clear. We don't
respect our fields; we lose patience with the slow
and sure of things; we kill the germs; we overheat
them; we arrange, we reason, we contrive. The
earth isn't a wife now; it's a kept woman!
And now, see how the enemy annihilates it!
Where it was wounded by the town,
'Tis burnt by war, the torch of war;
Where the wise man had wellnigh drained it dry,
The bullets fire it now.
Alas, alas, this is the death of it!
There is no need of rain or dewfall now,

14

THE DAWN

There is no need of snow about the mountain's head,
Nor yet of sun, nor of months clear and sweet,
And it were better at one stroke
To end, ending the country-side.

A PEASANT.
Truly, Old Ghislain is not sound in his head.

ANOTHER.
It is a crime to blaspheme the earth.

ANOTHER.
We do not know what to believe.
> [*The village Seer appears; he hums, imitat-
> ing by his gestures the flight of the fiery
> crows.*

THE SEER.
The forests fly and the meadow flows,
And the storm puts ruddy fingers forth
In crosses to the south and north.
It is the hour of the Fiery Crows.

They swoop on house and they sweep on hedge,
With frantic claws and wings stretched wide,
And with their burning plumes they fledge
The shifting skies on every side.

So swift they wing from banks and briars
Their unreturning passage out,
They seem the messengers of the fires
That ring the whole round world about.

Terror attends without a sound
The mystery of their silent flight;
Their beaks are sharp to rend the ground,
And savage there to ravage there
The very heart of earth from our delight.

15

THE DAWN

The seeds we sow, ere we have sown them, die,
The hayricks, with their leaping flames that wing
Their flying way towards the sunsetting,
Seem, in the smoke that whirls them high,
Like wild and bloody horses galloping.

This is the hour that was foretold.
Ho, bells! ho, bells! the bells have tolled;
Toll for the death of harvest, and the death of all.
This is the hour that was foretold.
Ho, the death-bells! ho, the death-bells! the bells
    have tolled;
Toll the death-bells for the world's funeral.

OLD GHISLAIN.
Ah well, it is he who is in the right, the seer, the
madman, he, whom we all mocked, whom I mocked
myself, and whom I have never understood. Ah, the
formidable light is there now. [*He points to the
horizon.*] But he knew it long ago. And we were
there, all of us, with an old hope, with our old illu-
sions, putting the poor little bar of our common-sense
between the spokes of the terrible wheels of destiny.

> [*A troop of young folks from the villages,
> farm labourers, workmen, stable-maids,
> beggars, carry forward* PIERRE HÉRÉ-
> NIEN *on a litter. A priest accompanies
> them. The dying man signs to them that
> he suffers too much, and that they must
> stop.*

JACQUES HÉRÉNIEN.
Here, my friends. Set him down gently. [*Helping
those who carry him. Then, as if speaking to himself.*]
Poor old man, poor old man! who could not die in
his bed, like his father! Oh, these wars, these wars,
they must be hated with a diamond-like hatred.

16

THE DAWN

PIERRE HÉRÉNIEN.
Hérénien, Hérénien!

JACQUES HÉRÉNIEN.
Here I am, father, close to you, close to your hands
and your eyes; close to you, as in the old times, as
in mother's times, so close, that I can hear your heart
beat. Do you see me? do you hear me? Do you
feel that it is I, and that I love you always?

PIERRE HÉRÉNIEN. [*Breathing heavily.*]
This time, it is the end. You will not be able to
carry me to your home, in Oppidomagne. I am
happy because the plains are all about me. I have
one favour to ask of you, that you do not forbid the
old curé to come to me.

JACQUES HÉRÉNIEN.
My father, you shall be obeyed in every will and
wish. Shall I go further off?

PIERRE HÉRÉNIEN.
I must be alone to confess.
          [HÉRÉNIEN *goes aside. The priest approaches.*
              OLD GHISLAIN *accosts the tribune*
              timidly. He speaks to him during the
              confession.

OLD GHISLAIN.
Monsieur Hérénien, I see you are always good. I
thought otherwise. You rule Oppidomagne, and in
our farms we talk of you. My sons defend you.
Perhaps they are right. But tell me, now that the
country is dead, how are we going to live? Where
shall we find a corner to sow the seed, and grow the

corn? Where shall we find an acre that the smoke
and the sewers and the poisons and the war have not
spoilt? tell me, tell me!

> [HÉRÉNIEN *remains silent. His whole atten-
> tion is given to his father. He merely
> shrugs his shoulders slightly when* OLD
> GHISLAIN *has done speaking.*

THE SHEPHERD. [*Who has slowly approached* HÉRÉ-
NIEN.]
Jacques, do you remember me?

JACQUES HÉRÉNIEN.
What! you are still alive, old shepherd?
> [*Embraces him with great emotion.*

THE SHEPHERD.
I went a great way off, yonder, for years; I have
seen new and marvellous countries. One wanders
on like that, from day to day, from moor to moor,
and one gets back in time to see someone die!

PIERRE HÉRÉNIEN.
I ask pardon of all whom I have offended.

THE CURÉ.
Do not be troubled, you were a christian, you will
be saved.   [*The priest absolves him.*

JACQUES HÉRÉNIEN. [*Leading the shepherd up to the
dying man.*]
Father, this is the shepherd; you know him well, the
shepherd of "Tinkling Meadow," the oldest of your
servants and of your friends.

THE DAWN

PIERRE HÉRÉNIEN. [*Looking for a long time at the shepherd, and then, all of a sudden, recognizing him, seizing his arm, and drawing him towards him. In almost a firm voice.*]
When I am dead, shepherd, destroy all the old seeds. They are full of evil germs; they are rotten; they are mouldy. It is not with them that the soil shall have its espousals. And you, who have been everywhere, you shall sow new seed in my fields and in my meadows; living seed, fresh seed, good seed that you have seen and found good, yonder, in the virgin countries of the earth. [*A pause. The shepherd bows his head and kneels. The beggars and the porters do the same.*] And now turn me to the sun.
> [*He is obeyed; but in the west, where the sun is then going down, the burning villages illuminate the country. The heat reaches to the dying man.*

A PEASANT. [*Pointing to* PIERRE HÉRÉNIEN.]
The shadow of the fire passes over his face.

ANOTHER.
He turns to the fire.

ANOTHER. [*To those about* PIERRE HÉRÉNIEN.]
Take care, take care, he must not see the flames.

ANOTHER.
Turn him to the right.

ANOTHER.
This way, this way, to the right, to the right.
> [*But the old man clings to the litter, and raises himself, his face towards the setting sun and the fires.*

THE DAWN

ANOTHER.
Poor man! if he knew!

PIERRE HÉRÉNIEN. [*In a scarcely audible voice.*]
Jacques Hérénien, come close to me, close. Let me
die touching you with my fingers [*he caresses him*],
and looking that way with my eyes at what I have
loved most in the world. I have loved you to dis-
traction; I have never denied you; I have almost
blessed the sorrows that you have given me; and,
while I have loved you, I have loved the earth. I
have lived with the sun, as with God; it was the
visible master of things. It would have been like a
punishment if I had died in the night, in its absence.
Happily, it is there before me, and I reach out my
arms to it. [*He lifts himself towards the conflagration.*]
I can see it no longer, but I still feel the good, conquering light.

JACQUES HÉRÉNIEN. [*Murmurs.*]
Father! father!
> [*Not knowing whether he should disabuse
> his father, or see in these words a sud-
> den prediction.*

PIERRE HÉRÉNIEN.
I feel it, I love it, I understand; it is from there,
now, that the only springtides now possible must
come!
> [*He falls back, and dies:* JACQUES HÉRÉ-
> NIEN *embraces his father, pressing his
> lips on his mouth as if he would gather
> the first truth that has ever left them.*

JACQUES HÉRÉNIEN.
Did he know what he was saying? "The only
springtides now possible!"
> [*Slowly* HÉRÉNIEN *returns to himself out of*

THE DAWN

his reverie. The beggars, peasants, and workmen surround him. The shepherd holds his hands and draws him close. The porters raise the body and move onward. At this moment a troop of women and children coming from the city turn into the open space from the upper roads. It is led by old men.

AN OLD MAN. [*Stopping and pointing to* PIERRE HÉRÉNIEN.]
A dead man! and Hérénien following the bier!

ANOTHER.
And this crowd?

ANOTHER.
It is the whole country-side flocking towards Oppidomagne.

ANOTHER.
Do they suppose they will be welcome there? [*He calls.*] Hérénien! Hérénien!

HÉRÉNIEN.
Who calls me?

THE OLD MAN.
Oppidomagne has shut itself in within its walls; it will not permit the plain to send it its vagabonds and its dead!

HÉRÉNIEN.
I am returning home; I have lost my father; I wish to bury him myself, and withdraw him from pillage and profanation.

THE DAWN

THE OLD MAN.
They will drive you back with bullets, they are
turning out all who do not help in the defences.

ANOTHER OLD MAN.
They are blowing up the bridges. The ramparts
are bristling with troops.

ANOTHER.
The city no longer knows whom it casts out. No
one will recognize you.

ANOTHER.
It is mad to go that way.

ANOTHER.
It is risking your life.

ANOTHER. [*Entreatingly.*]
Stay with us, among us. You will save us.

HÉRÉNIEN.
I swear to you that I will enter Oppidomagne. If
you doubt, follow me.

AN OLD MAN.
We cannot.

A PEASANT.
Better die in our own homes.
> [*The beggars, the old men, and some peasants
> remain. The rest follow* HÉRÉNIEN.
> *The funeral train disappears slowly.*

AN OLD MAN.
Hérénien is the only man still firm and stable, in
these hours of suspended thunder. Perhaps, after
all, they will welcome him.

THE DAWN

ANOTHER.
As for those who follow him, they will all be killed.

ANOTHER. [*Turning towards the country.*]
Look yonder; the enemy teaches the elements to
make war. He encircles them, deploys them, masters
them, throws them forward.

ANOTHER.
And the country once dead, they will destroy the
cities.

AN OLD MAN OF THE TOWNS. [*Older than the
    others.*]
O these cities! these cities!
And their tumults and their outcries
And their wild furies and their insolent attitudes
Against the brotherhood of men;
O these cities! and their wrath against the skies,
And their most terrible, most bestial, show,
And their stocked market of old sins,
And their vile shops,
Where wreathe, in knots of golden grapes,
All the unclean desires,
As, on a time, garlands of flowery breasts
Wreathed the white bodies of Diana's maids!
These cities!
The sense of youth is withered up in them;
The sense of heroism is sapped in them;
The sense of justice, as a useless thing, is cast away
    from them.
O these cities! these cities!
That spread themselves abroad like heaps of rotten-
    ness,
Like soft or vehement breeds of slime
Whose mouths and suckers wait to suck
The noble blood of all the world!

THE DAWN

A Peasant. [*To the old men.*]
Without you, the people of cities, our harvests would
flourish, our barns would run over with corn! Without you, we should still be strong, healthy, and
tranquil; without you, our daughters would not be
prostitutes, nor our sons soldiers. You have soiled
us with your ideas and with your vices, and it is
you who let loose war upon us.

One from the Towns. [*To the peasants.*]
It is of you that we should complain. Why do you
flock in, so many and so greedy? From your fields
you hasten to us to traffic with us, to steal from us,
and with so stubborn a mind, so narrow, so bitter,
and so violent a soul, that you are scarcely to be
distinguished from bandits. You have set your
malice and your thievishness behind all our counters.
You have cumbered little by little all the desks of
the world. If the age grinds its teeth with a great
noise of meddling and servile pens, it is your millions
of hands that were willing to copy till death.

One from the Villages.
You had need of us. You filled our plains with your
appeals.

One from the Towns.
You are the dough that mediocrity kneads, the
regiments that nullity numbers. You are the cause
of slow usury, idleness, and sluggishness. Without
you, the city would still be nervous, light, valiant;
without you, surprise, vivacity, daring might have
come back again. Without you, slumber would not
have paralysed life, nor death soaked space with
blood.

24

THE DAWN

AN OLD MAN.
Eh, but say now, do you think the enemy is waiting
all this time, with folded arms, until you have settled
your disputes? If our city perishes, certainly we
might swathe it in a shroud woven of all the needless words, of all the meaningless discussions, of all
the loquacity and eloquence, lavished upon it for
centuries. The talkers are the only guilty ones.

ANOTHER.
Everything has conspired against Oppidomagne.
There are a thousand causes which ruin it, as there
are a thousand worms that attack a corpse. Happily
there is always some Christ, far off, on the horizon.

ANOTHER.
Yesterday, the gravest insurrection terrified the city.
The people took refuge in the cemetery, which
overlooks the old quarters. The tombs served for
ramparts. They are on strike. The Regent's soldiers
surround it and cut it off.

A PEASANT.
Oppidomagne is besieged, then, and besieging.

THE OLD MAN.
As they did at Rome, the crowd has made an
Aventine.

ANOTHER.
O the foul shame of being one of this degraded race,
Whose mortal and whose trumpeting wantonness
Affrights the very reason of the earth.
Now in these hours of thunder in the air,
Instead of setting to,
Now at the last, to seek for strength out of the
    common strength,

25

THE DAWN

It falls apart, it spreads abroad, it drops away.
Say, is there then no longer some unwavering light,
Is there no longer then an axiom of aught,
Is there no longer a strong hand with us
To scourge the wandering flock of these soft wills
    of ours?
Say, is there then a man no more?
        [*The village Seer, who has never ceased
            roaming to and fro, prophesies.*

THE SEER.
The times which were to come have come at last,
Wherein the city, long the mirror of all eyes,
The marvellous mirror that had glassed
The eyes of the world,
Scatters the glory of its memories.

Oppidomagne!
With thy quays, columns, bridges, thy triumphal
    arch,
Behold against thy pride
The whole horizons march!

Oppidomagne!
With thy towers, monuments, belfries, far and wide,
Behold in blood of fire written upon thy walls
The sign and seal of funerals!

Oppidomagne! Now is the hour
When all things fixed shall crumble into sand,
Unless without delay,
This day,
Some mighty one puts forth his hand!

AN OLD MAN.
Oh, whoever he is, how we shall all shout for him,
and how we shall be the first to bow down to him!

26

THE DAWN

THE SEER.
This one that we await
Shall be so great,
That needs must all you rise to him, maybe
If you would know that this indeed is he.

AN OLD MAN.
He is not yet born.

ANOTHER.
No one can guess him.

ANOTHER.
No one proclaims him.

ANOTHER.
And Jacques Hérénien?

ANOTHER.
Jacques Hérénien? He is mad!

SCENE II

*As the curtain rises, a cordon of cavalry bars the
gate to Oppidomagne. The soldiers are at work
undermining the bridges across the river. Patrols
mount guard on the slope and the ramparts. A
general, field-glass in hand, inspects the horizon.
He watches what is going on, while a messenger
runs up, handing an order to the officer in command
of the cavalry.*

THE OFFICER. [*Reading.*]
"Orders are given to admit no one into the city;
except the tribune Jacques Hérénien. It is important

27

THE DAWN

that he should realize the favour that is shown him.
He is to be opposed as a matter of form.

      (Signed)   The Regency of Oppidomagne."

*[Hérénien appears on the main road, followed
by the crowd of ragged men, woman,
workmen, farmers, and old men. Finding that entry will be difficult, he advances by himself to the officer.*

HÉRÉNIEN.

I am of those who must be heard. Oppidomagne is
the city where I have grown up, suffered, fought for
my ideas, which are the greatest that a man can bear
about with him. I loved Oppidomagne when it
seemed invincible. To-day I desire my place among
those who die for her. And I desire the like for all
those who are here, for all whom I have met with
on the way. It is I who have called them to follow
me. I have turned back towards courage the flood
that was going down to cowardice.

THE OFFICER.

I know who you are, but I cannot alter the orders
I have received.

HÉRÉNIEN.

What are the orders?

THE OFFICER.

To keep that barrier shut.

          [He points to the gate of the city.

HÉRÉNIEN.

Then it must be that this Oppidomagne,
At the tremendous hour
When mountainous woe and terror fall upon its pride,

28

THE DAWN

With the mere poor and little words of a command
Shuts to its gates,
Shuts from its door
Those that are bringing it
Their blood, their hearts,
And the most vehement flame of all their loves!
I, who so oft at night-time, at the harbour-side,
Have seen the seas
Press on and cast abroad in it
The formidable and free universe,
Even I who love her, be she evil or good,
I who so strangely love, I who so blindly love,
That I am as a son, yet passionate as a lover,
I must go forth from her, and like a hunted beast!
An order! But it is such orders that ruin a people.
Do you reckon up the number of defenders when
the sorrow is infinite? Do you separate for death
those that the same danger unites? I insist that you
make room for all.

THE OFFICER.
Impossible.

[HÉRÉNIEN *goes up to the corpse of his father,
and uncovers his head and shoulders.*

HÉRÉNIEN.
For twenty years this man there was a soldier;
He served your leaders over the whole earth,
He has fought at the poles, in the desert, and on the
       sea;
Thrice he has crossed Europe from end to end
In a tempestuous cloud
Of frantic flags and golden eagles and great lights!
Is it to him you close the gates of Oppidomagne?

THE OFFICER.
To all who are with you.

29

THE DAWN

HÉRÉNIEN.
Know, then, that it is in the name of the clearest, simplest, most unvarying law that I appeal to your honour as a man. In a few days this plain will be ruin, putrefaction, and blood. You have a mere word to say, and all our lives, to which we all have a right, will be saved. The help that men owe to men, you who bear arms, you first of all owe to us. This duty wipes out all others. There was a time when the very name of army and of watchword was unknown.

THE OFFICER.
Disperse, disperse.

HÉRÉNIEN. [*He looks towards the vast crowd which follows him, reckons up the number of soldiers with a glance, and goes up to his dead father.*]
I ask the pardon of this dead man for desecrating his funeral with blood.

> [*At this moment the general, who observes the scene from the height of the rampart, approaches the officer.*

HÉRÉNIEN. [*To the crowd.*]
I have used all means, there remains but one. You all know it. We are a thousand, and these, but a few. [*Pointing to the soldiers.*] Some among them have fathers and children among you. They are ours; they will let us pass. Let the women come forward: they will not fire on them. [*Advancing alone, while the crowd forms in order. To the soldiers.*] He who commands you bids you commit a crime. Disobey him. The right is yours.

> [*Already the general has rejoined the officer, and reprimands him. The words " stupidity " and " folly " are heard. The general advances rapidly towards* HÉRÉNIEN *and salutes him.*

30

THE DAWN

THE GENERAL.
Jacques Hérénien, enter Oppidomagne. The Regency bids you welcome.

HÉRÉNIEN.
At last! I knew that you had need of me, and that
it is in your interest that I come into your midst.
[*Pointing to the crowd.*] And all these follow me;
the old men, the children, the women, they shall all
return home, they will all be useful. And you, my
father, you shall rest in the tomb where my two
children sleep already.

> [*The general makes no objeĉtion. The ranks
> open. JACQUES HÉRÉNIEN and some
> workmen enter the city, but no sooner
> have they passed than suddenly, at the
> officer's command, the ranks close. The
> body of PIERRE HÉRÉNIEN, the porters,
> the old men, the peasants, the women and
> the children are thrust back. Fresh
> battalions hastening up lend their aid.
> JACQUES HÉRÉNIEN, astonished, turns
> to make his way back. He is heard to
> cry: "Cowardice," "Treason," "In-
> famy." But the tumult covers his voice.
> He is violently hurried into the city.
> And the howling crowd is driven back
> into the plain.*

ACT II

Scene I

HÉRÉNIEN's *house. Door to* R.; *commonplace furniture;
stove at back. Things lying about pell-mell. On
the table, clothes that are being mended, children's
toys. Heaps of books on the chairs.* CLAIRE,
HÉRÉNIEN's *wife, finishes lighting the lamps. She
waits. All at once there is a noise of cheering in
the street.* HÉRÉNIEN *enters. He clasps his wife
in a long embrace.*

HÉRÉNIEN.

WE have buried my father to the left of the
little ones, under the yew-tree which overlooks our burial-place. He will rest there as he did
in the village; his body will mingle with the ele-
mentary life of the herbs and plants that he loved so
much.

CLAIRE.
Did they spy on you?
    [*During this scene* HÉRÉNIEN *changes his
     black clothes for indoor things. Impres-
     sion of home.*

HÉRÉNIEN.
I don't know. There were only a few of us. On
the way back, we passed the crowd; newsboys were
calling the news of the Aventine. Everybody made

for the papers. Some men carried torches and sang. Along the boulevards and avenues houses lay open, split or pierced by the bombs. The rubbish was all over the pavements. Not a single gas-lamp was lighted. At the National Place a quarry-man called my name: that was all. When they allowed me to bring my father into Oppidomagne—after God knows what difficulties!—I promised that he should be buried without any crowd of people. I have kept my word. [*Finding a roll of banknotes on the writing-desk.*] What is this?

CLAIRE.
They have sent the remainder of the account. [*Taking a note out of her pocket.*] Look. Your last book has been read everywhere.

HÉRÉNIEN. [*Looking at the letter.*]
They must read and discuss me; they must hunger and thirst after my justice! [*He puts the letter on the table, and opens the window. Going nearer to* CLAIRE.] I thought of us, during that simple and homely funeral. I would like to have felt you by my side, when the coffin sank into the earth! My heart was so tortured, so full of pent-up tenderness, so walled up within myself. Why had I not your hands in mine, to mark there the half of my mourning! [*He takes her hand.*] You are indeed my sweet and valiant one. You know me, you understand me, before you alone I dare be without compunction what I truly am: a poor human being, seldom calm, full of vehement pride and tenderness, the more exacting because I love the more. Where is the boy?

CLAIRE. [*Points to the room at the* R.]
In our room, asleep.

33   D

THE DAWN

HÉRÉNIEN.

How often I drove my father to despair! My fits
and starts of will were so wild that he used to beat
me, and I cried out under his blows, and shrieked,
and yelled at him all the same just what I pleased.
And now to-day I would strangle my son if he were
to irritate me. [*A shell bursts not far from the house.*
HÉRÉNIEN *and* CLAIRE *rush to the window. The
crowd applauds* HÉRÉNIEN.] This, now, is the best
time to love. There is nothing like these crises and
alarms for bringing people closer together. I seem
to see you in the first months of our love; you seem
to me even more beautiful; I bring you my love just
as sincere, just as ardent, just as absolute as ever.

CLAIRE.

And I love and serve you with all my soul.

HÉRÉNIEN.

This funeral (in which some part of myself has gone,
I know not what, a part of my life, my childhood)
tore me away from my burning existence, given up
to all, taken by all, scattered wide, far from you,
far from us, all through Oppidomagne. I seemed to
myself to be in the village, in the desolate land of the
visionary plains; prowling, at night, on the heath,
or astride of the wild colts in my father's fields. I
remembered the shepherds, the servants, the maid-
servants. I remembered the way to school, to church,
and the exact sound of the parish bell. I was so sad
and so happy; I longed to see you again, you and
the child. [*Putting his arm round* CLAIRE.] And
now, let me see your eyes, your pale, sweet eyes,
that love me more than all others, and are the fairest
lights in the world. [*Leaning his face over* CLAIRE.]
Are they not faithful, and tender, and peaceful, and

34

shining, and am I not foolish to make them weep sometimes?

CLAIRE.
Your words go further than your thoughts, when they are unkind.

HÉRÉNIEN.
Oh! I am not one of those who love tamely. But you, you love me all the same, although you know my terrible life, my real life, my real reason of being on the earth.

CLAIRE. [*With a slight tone of reproach.*]
You talk to me of that so often!

HÉRÉNIEN.
And I will talk of it to you again; I will be brutal, and weary you, because it is my passion to be absolutely sincere with you. You would be my wife no longer, if I had to hide anything from you. I would rather see you weep than lie to you.

CLAIRE.
If you were otherwise, I should love you the less.

HÉRÉNIEN.
And besides, you know very well that I exaggerate; that really, when I assign you so small a space in my life, I deceive myself and you.

CLAIRE.
Ah, be what you will, tormentor or despot, what does it matter? You belong to me, you and our child, to all my love.

HÉRÉNIEN.
Ah, you indeed are my wife!
When, on a night of June,

35

THE DAWN

Long ago now, sweetly you gave me your soul,
Did I not swear that my lips
Never again should kiss
Another's lips,
Another's breast?
You were the flower of all the lakes and mists
That my impetuous hands
Have wrested from my haggard country
And planted in the heart of Oppidomagne;
And 'tis the soil, the waters, and the meadow-lands,
That I behold and worship in your naked eyes.
And shall not we remain, hand in hand, heart to
      heart,
Lost in the love that sets us free,
Adoringly, forgivingly, exultingly,
While the insatiable days eat up the time
Our fates shall let us live?
Death like a fire enrings us round about,
Night is an ambush set, and evening a disaster;
And see, in the insensate skies,
The stars hurtle together and consume,
And the hot fiery ashes fall!

> [HÉRÉNIEN's *child comes in to embrace his
> father, who hardly notices and seems to
> have forgotten him. The crowd goes by,
> with vociferous shouting.* HÉRÉNIEN
> *rushes to the window. Shouts are heard.
> "The Exchange is on fire!" "The
> Arsenal is on fire!" "The Port is on
> fire!" The reflection of the flames
> illuminates the room.*

HÉRÉNIEN.
And what if this indeed ended Oppidomagne!
And if these bonfires emptied from their mountain-
      tops

THE DAWN

The smoking blood of sacrifice?
Oppidomagne
Has gathered to its codes and ratified in laws
All that was once a hidden crime, a crafty murder,
Deceit or theft against true justice and true good.
And now that it is puffed and sated with its vices,
And drunk enough to drink the very dregs
That foul its gutters to the brim,
All the dull evils, all the muddy lusts,
Hang at its girdle, night and day,
And drain its breasts, like hungering wolves.
If then these palaces, these sheds,
If these bright arsenals, if these gloomy temples, fall,
Crumble to shameful dust,
The world will shout to see the red sparks fly,
To meet the future half way, on the wind.
But that the city itself should have an end,
Being the soul of future things,
That these should sink under the waves of flame;
That the tied bundle of our fates
She in her hands yet holds,
Break in the furious feeble hands,
Break now, and break in face of death;
That the fair gardens of to-morrow
Whose gates she opened wide
Be wasted with the thunderbolt,
And cumbered with dead things;
It is impossible: he is mad who says it.
Oppidomagne, with all her happy hopes,
With all her beacons triumphing in the night,
Shall stand, shall stand erect,
As long as any men, whose faith is like my faith,
Have blood in them to shed, that faith bear fruit
      in them,
And that the blind and greedy world at length
Be fashioned to the will of the new gods!

THE DAWN

CLAIRE.
Oh! the terrors and the sorrows that we shall have
to endure!

HÉRÉNIEN.
Whatever they may be, I forbid you to complain of
them. We live in formidable days of terrors, agonies,
and new births. The unknown becomes the master.
Men shake with an immense movement of the head
the weight of all the errors of ages. Utopia resigns
its wings, and takes root in the earth. Our very
besiegers know of it.

CLAIRE.
Had you any news of the enemy this morning?

HÉRÉNIEN.
Not yet; but what the captain, Hordain, predicted
yesterday, gave me fire and flame for weeks and
weeks. This captain belongs to the race of men who
realize the impossible. Think! he and I, to kill the
war dead, here, before the discharged and powerless
chiefs! To bring about the public reconciliation of
the foreign soldiers and ours! To exhaust all the
forces of one's being, all the energies of one's faith,
for that supreme end! What a splendid dream!

CLAIRE. [*Gently ironical.*]
What a delusion!

HÉRÉNIEN.
We should never reject a hope when it spreads such
wings. What remains improbable to-day, will be
accomplished fact to-morrow. Hordain relies so far
only on dim surmisings, a deep but stifled discontent,
secret understandings and unions. The troops refuse

38

THE DAWN

to fight; they are tired out; they disband. Ideas of
justice are in the air. There is vague talk of concord ;
the spark is set to the grate. I await the breath of
wind that shall set the wood and straw alight.

> [HÉRÉNIEN *listens to the murmurs in the
> street. There is a knock at the door. The
> Consul of Oppidomagne enters the room.*

THE CONSUL.

Jacques Hérénien, I come to you in the name of the
Regency of Oppidomagne, to ask you to accomplish
a great duty. Far as our ideas are from one another,
an understanding between us is certain, when it is a
question of saving the city. I seem to speak to the
future leader of this people that we love in different
ways, but both of us ardently.

HÉRÉNIEN.

Preambles are useless. I ask what brings you, and
what you expect of me.

> [*He motions to the Consul to sit down.*

THE CONSUL.

Up yonder, at the cemetery, the situation of your
friends is lamentable. They would not resist a
serious attack; yesterday the Regency was anxious
to bring them to order; but they seem to be numerous, young, hardy; they are needed for the defence
of Oppidomagne. Up to now, they were scarcely
rebels; they are disaffected, on strike: that is all.
To-morrow, when they have seen the terrible con-
flagrations that are spreading yonder, perhaps they
will in turn become incendiaries. Hate counsels folly,
and if they slay and pillage, it will not indeed be the
end of things, but it will be an end in shame.

39

THE DAWN

HÉRÉNIEN.

I hold war in execration. This between men of the same soil terrifies me more than any other. You, in Oppidomagne, have moved heaven and earth to bring it about. You have cultivated the misery of the people; you have refused it bread, justice, dignity; you have tyrannized it in its body and in its thought; you have helped yourselves with its ignorance, as with your disloyalty, your cleverness, your lying, your irony, and your contempt. You are unworthy and culpable.

THE CONSUL.

I believed you to have a more balanced, a more un-clouded, and a loftier judgement.

HÉRÉNIEN.

I think and judge before you, as I would think and judge before the enemy. I hate, but pity you.

THE CONSUL. [*Rising.*]
This is an outrage.

HÉRÉNIEN.
It is passion and frankness.

THE CONSUL.
It is above all injustice.

HÉRÉNIEN.

Come now! But shall I ever end if I begin to show you the anger of the cities and the dread of the country?
My memory is faithful: it is armed
With those remembrances that shall cut deep as
    sickles.
It reckons up the murders you and yours have done,

40

THE DAWN

It knows the soul you bear, and it defies you
To be but honest, loyal, just,
Or, without vice, strong in your strength.
But I forget myself to thus instruct you,
Knowing that you will turn again
To weave your spiders' web of twisted perfidy.
Treachery is a sacred thing
For all of you: it holds you, hunts you, binds you up
Within a monstrous and most fatal forfeiture.

THE CONSUL.
You have then no confidence?

HÉRÉNIEN.
None.

THE CONSUL.
Then, I retire.   [*The Consul rises to leave.*

HÉRÉNIEN.
I wait. . . .
                [*The Consul hesitates, takes two steps, and
                changes his mind.*

THE CONSUL.
Come, it would be folly to let our words get the
better of our deeds. Oppidomagne alone should
occupy us.

HÉRÉNIEN.
I had no other thought when I received you here.

THE CONSUL.
A man of affairs and intelligence, such as you are,
knows better than anyone how we have spread
abroad the name and influence of Oppidomagne.

THE DAWN

Its history is the history of its Regents
And of its Consuls, who, 'neath skies of flaming gold,
Across red soil that lighted up with blood,
Unto the end of the world,
Drew after them its host with their magnetic hand.
Our troubles, in these times, were many and were
    fruitful.
The people and its leaders both
Were rivals in the battle-field. And those,
Yonder, who threaten and lay siege to us,
Know what a crimson and triumphant fluttering,
Once, our insatiate flags,
Flung to the winds upon their plains of snow.
Oppidomagne is splendid in the eyes of all,
Oppidomagne is vaster than the memory
The sea and earth and wind and sun have kept of it;
Crime, and the noble deeds of war, divide its glory;
You only see, you only speak, its crimes.

HÉRÉNIEN.
Your glory is all ended, it has stooped to earth;
With its illustrious sword itself has slain the right;
To-day another glory comes about,
Another rises in my breast,
Perfect and strong and virginal of stain.
And this glory is made up of the new and profound
justice, of private heroism, of ardent tenacity, of
necessary and temporary violence. It is less brilliant
than yours, but surer. The whole world awaits it.
Both of us, you with fear and I with fervour, feel it
to be inevitable and imminent. That is why you
come to me; that is why I have the temerity to
treat you as though you were already conquered.
Do what you will, you and your caste, you are, at
this moment, the prisoners of my consent or my
refusal.

42

THE DAWN

THE CONSUL.
You mistake. . . .

HÉRÉNIEN.
No! Like me, you know well that you can do nothing without my aid. In my hands, I hold [all the deep moral force of Oppidomagne.

THE CONSUL.
You forget what the ruin of an empire would mean. All the ancient interests, all the customs of ages, sustain it. And we have with us the army.

HÉRÉNIEN.
The army? Say rather, the chiefs; for the soldiers hesitate or protest. They are on the eve of joining the people. They are my hope and your fear. If they all obeyed you, if you did not fear an immense insurrection, the people and the soldiers together, you would have already bombarded the Aventine. [*A silence.*] Well, you come to ask me, do you not, to go up yonder, to the mountain, among the tombs, and enjoin on those oppressed people to come down into the midst of those who have enslaved them. Oh! I see all the danger and the peril of my mission!

THE CONSUL.
You are mistaken. The Regency begs you to announce that the hour has come when perils are so great as to overcome all rancour. Whoever believes in Oppidomagne should turn hero. Our people has unknown possibilities of regeneration.

HÉRÉNIEN.
How would they be treated if they came down from up yonder?

43

THE DAWN

THE CONSUL.
The soldiers should return to their proper rank in the army, the others should return to their homes and families. If poverty, since they have left, has crept in, it shall be banished. For the rest, promise what you will: you are loyal. We have confidence in you.

HÉRÉNIEN.
Will you sign that for me?

THE CONSUL.
It is done. [*Hands him a written paper.*] Read.
[HÉRÉNIEN *goes over it and appears satisfied.*

HÉRÉNIEN.
One last word. When I brought after me the farmers of the villages, the old men and vagabonds of the cities, why were they driven back from the walls, towards the enemy?

THE CONSUL.
It was an error. You should have been listened to.

HÉRÉNIEN.
And who allowed me to bury my father among his own folk?

THE CONSUL.
I myself.

HÉRÉNIEN.
Go then, and tell the Regency that I will go to the Aventine.

> [HÉRÉNIEN *goes to the window and cries to the people still standing in the street:* "*Let the man who comes out of my house pass without a murmur: he has done his duty. . . . To-night, at the cemetery, yonder!*"

44

THE DAWN

At the Aventine (cemetery on a height). People assem-
bled, HAINEAU *occupies the tribune: a tomb higher*
than the others. Stacked arms are planted among
the little funereal gardens. Crosses, small pillars,
pedestals, and columns emerge from among the
flowers. On the wall surrounding it armed work-
men are on guard. Night is coming on. Fires are
lighted.

HAINEAU.
I conclude then, as I concluded yesterday: in a
revolution it is essential to strike at ideas in the person of those who represent them. It is essential to go
slowly, not to be carried away, and to make for immediate ends. Coldly, each of us will choose his man,
his victim. No one shall lie down to rest until the
three Regents and the two Consuls of Oppidomagne
are dead. It is the work of terror that brings the
work of safety.

THE CROWD.
—Why proclaim what should be kept quiet?
—Every man is master of his own knife.
—Silence!

HAINEAU.
The enemy burns the churches, the banks, the
parliaments. The Capitol and the Regency remain.
Let us destroy them. Let us go down by night, in
bands, into Oppidomagne.

SOMEONE.
Impossible, the Aventine is surrounded.

45

THE DAWN

HAINEAU.
Someone can always be bought over.

THE CROWD.
—What is the use of these massacres?
—One chief dies, and another takes his place.
—We should conquer the whole mass.

HAINEAU.
You must cut off his head if you would master the beast. Once upon a time, in Oppidomagne, when we protested among ourselves, who dreamed of half-measures? Then we used to admire those who swept away things and people. Banks and theatres were blown up, and fearless, unflinching, the admirable assassins of old ideas died; they seemed to the judges madmen, but to the people heroes. That was the time of ingenuous sacrifices, tragical decisions, swift executions. Contempt of life swept over the universe. Now to-day everything is flabby and flaccid: energy is like an unstrung bow. We prevaricate, wait, reason, calculate; and you fear Oppidomagne conquered, though you dared it when it was conquering.

THE CROWD.
—We love it now that it is besieged.
—Our wives and children are there still.
—Our strike will come to nothing.
—Let us go back to Oppidomagne.

HAINEAU.
When you will anything, you must will it in spite of everything. The hour of the last anguish has come. What matter the sorrows and the sobs of our mothers if, thanks to our sufferings, new life is gained!

46

THE DAWN

SOMEONE. [*Pointing to* HAINEAU.]
He has no children!

HAINEAU.
If I had, I would sacrifice them for the future.

SOMEONE.
These are only words: you draw back when the
time comes for action.

HAINEAU.
I have approved myself during the time of the revolt.

SOMEONE.
You hid yourself when they were killing the people.

HAINEAU.
If I had the thousand arms of a crowd, I would act
alone, and I would disdain you. . . .
[*Hooting and jostling :* HAINEAU *is dislodged
from the tribune.*

A GROUP IN THE CROWD.
—There goes another who won't make fools of us
any more.
—He is too base and cowardly.

ANOTHER GROUP.
—We loathe him, now that we know ourselves
better.
—We don't know what we want, now that we want
it all together.
—If we don't do something we are lost.
—Let us go back to Oppidomagne.
[*The tumult quiets down.* LE BREUX *mounts
the tribune.*

47

THE DAWN

LE BREUX.
Haineau let himself be carried away for nothing.
He accused us of lacking daring. Is not our very
presence on this mountain sufficient proof of heroism?
At any moment we may be attacked and cut to
pieces.

HAINEAU.
Take care; you will frighten them.

LE BREUX. [*Shrugging his shoulders, glancing at*
HAINEAU, *and continuing.*]
We must not use up, on ourselves and among ourselves, the hate that should strike only Oppidomagne.
We have now been here together for a week, and already divisions, jealousies, spite, the hesitation of one,
the folly of another, get the better of our mutual understanding, cemented though it was by God knows
what promises! Happily, I have good news for you.
The Regency authorizes Hérénien to treat with us
here on the Aventine. [*Showing a written paper.*
His letter brings me the announcement.

THE CROWD. [*On all sides.*]
—Hérénien will see clear. It is he who overcomes
all our troubles.
—He knows what to do.
—He will give us back to ourselves.

AN OPPONENT.
Must he always be called on?

ANOTHER.
We abandon ourselves to him like women.

LE BREUX.
You tempt the people by speaking like that.

48

THE DAWN

AN OPPONENT.
We open its eyes; we put it on its guard against
itself.

LE BREUX.
The crowd adores Hérénien. It does not discuss its
enthusiasms.

AN OPPONENT.
Hérénien is not a God. Why did he leave Oppidomagne on the night of the revolt?

LE BREUX.
His father was dying.

AN OPPONENT.
His leaving was a mask for his flight. Hérénien pays
you to defend him.

LE BREUX.
If I was in his pay, you would have been in mine
long ago. You have a little low soul which cannot
understand a higher one than your own.
                              [*Acclamations.*

SOMEONE.
Let us wait for Hérénien.

A YOUNG MAN.
I will follow him, but I will kill him if he betrays
us.

LE BREUX.
I answer for him, as you answer for yourself to
yourself. We need Hérénien. We are sure of him.
Look yonder. [*There is a movement near the gate of*

THE DAWN

the cemetery.] He is coming. It is only he who is
strong enough to unite us and save us.

> [*The crowd masses itself on the boundary
> wall. Long cheering.* HÉRÉNIEN
> *mounts rapidly on a tomb, and speaks,
> keeping his eye on* HAINEAU, *who is in
> front of him.*

HÉRÉNIEN.
At last I am with you! You and I are only half
alive, when we live apart. At the village where my
father died I heard of your exodus to this mountain.
I thought of Roman times, of the pride, the decisive-
ness, the courage, the beauty, of the supreme peoples.
Let what may come of it, this dazzling and brutal
act will have greatened you. You have proved your
combined stubbornness and your single valour.
Those that refuse to you, soldiers, your proper pay,
to you, citizens, complete justice, because you were
the claimants for it, are to-day checkmated. The
means you have used were excellent. But will they
remain so?
An armed conflict with Oppidomagne would be
a disaster. Up to now it has been postponed. Up
to now, you have remained bound together in an
admirable bond of defence. I affirm, before you all,
that you have been proud to live together, thanks
to your clear and mutual good-will. You have
realized that the future depended upon your attitude.
That is well. [*Silence. All heads are bowed.*] But
will this union maintain itself, in the midst of the
misery and the famine that will break out here?
[*General silence.* HAINEAU *shrugs his shoulders.*
HÉRÉNIEN *gathers that there has been a dispute.
Suddenly changing his tone.*] You were, I admit, in
terrible straits. From the height of this mountain of

THE DAWN

death, certainly, you dominated those whom you detested. But your hearths and homes were wanting; your wives were wanting, your sons, your daughters. The Regency held them in its grasp, already impatient to crush them out. Ah! you have suffered the interminable passing of black hours, the long and slow procession of anguish after anguish through the soul! Happily all may be changed. The Regency offers you peace.

HAINEAU.
Never will we parley with the Regents.

HÉRÉNIEN.
If you refuse to parley, the massacre begins. What! we are a handful of enthusiasts here, whose action will decide the lot of a people; we are on the eve of an enormous victory for the people, and we consent to die like a rat in a trap.   [*Cheers.*

HAINEAU.
Everything that comes from the Regency must be rejected without consideration.

HÉRÉNIEN.
Everything that it offers must be considered, and used for our own advantage. What matter the danger of the means! I am a man who would use the thunder itself!   [*Cheers.*

HAINEAU.
We shall be your dupes.

HÉRÉNIEN.
What do you know of my designs, of my hopes, of my life? You disorganize: I organize. Those who listen to you waste themselves in defiances, in plots,

in terrorizings. For a week now you have been
using your utmost rigour: you have achieved a
nullity, mere disputes. I come and I find your work
paltry. I am ashamed of it. [*Cheers.*

HAINEAU.
I will have no tyrant. [*Hooting.*

HÉRÉNIEN.
You would become one, if I let you. [*Cheers.*

HAINEAU.
You overturn the Regency only to usurp its place.

HÉRÉNIEN.
Its place! I might have taken it: I disdained it.
[*Cheers.*
HAINEAU.
You consent to the most dubious compromises, you
traffic. . . .

HÉRÉNIEN.
Silence! Not a word more! This debate shall not
descend to personal questions. [*Addressing himself
directly to the crowd.*] I hate the authorities to
such a degree that I do not so much as dictate to
you the conditions of peace. You yourselves shall
impose them upon the Regency. Speak. [*Cheers.*

SOMEONE.
We want to be treated as men. We have used our
rights in striking for them.

HÉRÉNIEN.
Perfect.

THE DAWN

ANOTHER.
We want our goods to be restored to us.

HÉRÉNIEN.
Promised.

ANOTHER.
We want the arrears of wages to be paid to work-men.

HÉRÉNIEN.
The Regency agrees to it.

ANOTHER.
We want to re-enter the town under arms.

HÉRÉNIEN.
You may. And I add: if confiscations have taken place during your absence, they shall be annulled. All condemnations shall be forgotten. You your-selves shall be the judges of those who have judged you. [*Cheers.*] And now that we are in agreement, tell me: would it not have been monstrous that men of the same soil should have cut one another's throats? Think: yonder, in the feverous streets of the old quarters, in the atmosphere of powder and conflagration, disabled folk have taken refuge, in an immense hope of some renewal. More and more it is our programmes that they discuss, our discourses that they comment on, our soul that they drink in. The army itself is in a ferment with our dreams. Every discontent, every grudge, every injustice, every oppression, every enslavement, takes an un-known voice to make itself heard! Our masters hate each other. They have no more strength. They obey a phantom. [*Acquiescence from all sides.*] Among

53

the enemy, the same confusion, the same weakness. Mutinies break out among the soldiers. There are revolts against the cruelty of chiefs, against the horrors and follies of the campaign. Storms of hatred arise. Sick of nameless dreads, distresses, and miseries, all long after the necessary union of man with man. They are ashamed to be butchers of their fellows. And now, if this conflagration of instincts could be extinguished; if our besiegers could be made to feel that they would find brotherly souls among us; if by a sudden understanding we might realize to-day a little of the great human dream, Oppidomagne would be forgiven for all its shame, its folly, its blasphemy; it would become the place in the world where one of the few sacred events had happened. It is with this thought that you must all follow me down, towards your children.

[Cheers.

THE CROWD.
—He is the only one who makes things move.
—Without him, our cause was lost.

SOMEONE. [*Speaking directly to* HÉRÉNIEN.]
We will all obey you; you, you are our master.

> [*Cheers. They hoist* HÉRÉNIEN *on their shoulders, and carry him towards the city.* LE BREUX *escorts him. All descend. Cries of triumph are heard.*

ACT III

Scene I

A fortnight after. Abode of HÉRÉNIEN, *the same as in the second act. The work-table, covered with papers, is near the window, in which panes are broken. In the streets, the crowd comes and goes, retires to a distance and returns; groups cry:* "*Down with the traitor!*" "*Death to the traitor!*" "*Death to him!*" "*Down with him!*"

CLAIRE.

AND now this has lasted for a fortnight! The house seems like a ship in distress. Billows of rage and shouting beat upon it. Oh! that accursed affair on the Aventine! To have fallen all of a sudden from the height of enthusiasm, into disgrace and hate!

[HAINEAU *enters rapidly.*

CLAIRE.
You! here!

HAINEAU.
Yes, I.

CLAIRE.
What do you want?

HAINEAU.
You don't know then of my speech in the "Old Market"? I expected a better welcome.

55

THE DAWN

CLAIRE. [*Pointing to* HÉRÉNIEN'S *room.*]
What, you! his adversary and his enemy! [*Pointing to the street.*] You who stir up those cries and uproars!

HAINEAU.
By this time, after what he must know, Hérénien will receive me better than you, my friend and my sister.

CLAIRE.
I do not understand.

HAINEAU.
You will understand soon. Meanwhile, tell me, what was he like during these days of vain and miserable rage?

CLAIRE.
Oh, do not think he is overcome! He is still splendidly erect; he is carrying out the boldest of projects: he will reconcile Oppidomagne with the enemy.

HAINEAU. [*Pointing to the street.*]
But these uproars at his door?

CLAIRE.
At first, it was hard. It was useless for me to espouse his furies, envelop him with my fervour, wait upon him better than ever: he called up all his old grudges, he stirred himself up to anger, he rushed to the window, shook his fist at the city, shouted with rage, and the tears started from his eyes. In all his violence he was the terrible child that you know.

THE DAWN

HAINEAU.
Ah! if he had only listened to me, we should never have fallen out. The Regency would not have deceived him. The people would love him still. But he is not to be disciplined: he has never known what it is to will patiently. He goes by bounds and tempests, like the winds of his country.

CLAIRE.
And what ought he to have done?

HAINEAU.
Prolonged the revolt on the Aventine; extended it instead of reducing it, accepted the civic conflict, made the misery sharper; seized the banks by force; the public services by force; destiny, by force.

CLAIRE.
It was impossible.

HAINEAU.
Everything was possible, in the state of fever in which we were. But there had to be a plan, a resolution coldly taken and followed. First, we should have organized the resistance: we were on strike, up yonder; then the attack; then the massacre. It was the immediate, definite, urgent things that needed seeing to. Those in authority would have been assassinated: Regent and Consuls. They were beginning to listen to me. Hérénien came to the Aventine at an unlucky moment: circumstances were in his favour. He is the sentimental tribune in speaking, big gestures, big words: he magnetizes, he does not convince. Ah! when I think of it, all my hatred comes back to me.

57

THE DAWN

CLAIRE.
How you deceive yourself!

[*Clamours in the street.* HAINEAU *and*
CLAIRE *pay no heed to them.*

HAINEAU.
He seems not to know what he wants himself. He
always looks beyond the hour. I never understand
him.

CLAIRE.
I always understand him.

HAINEAU.
It is a mistake to put all his will into the service of
certain dreams. He who blows down the tube too
hard breaks the glass.

CLAIRE.
Don't let us discuss things. You are violent, and you
feel that you are weak and ill at ease. If you are
here, in his house, it is to ask for something. What
is it?

HAINEAU. [*With pride.*]
I have come here to tell you that yesterday, I, I who
am now speaking, overcame the crowd, defended
Hérénien, made them cheer him. My tenacity has
conquered his ill-luck.

CLAIRE.
You have done that, you? But how then does your
conduct go with your ideas?

HAINEAU.
Ah, it is like this! When I act for myself, I am a
failure, I am betrayed, I am hated, Le Breux sup-

plants me; in short, Hérénien, in spite of all, is the only man who can save things, at the point they have reached. He has ravelled them, let him unravel them.

CLAIRE.
And you, you have sustained him.

HAINEAU.
Certainly, because we cannot have the revolt over again, because everything crumbles through my fingers, because I have no chance, no luck. If I could only tell you how childish the people are, and how they are already regretting that they have no master! Oh! it is all over, it is all over! and one ought to have the strength to disappear.

CLAIRE.
It is in despair then that you sustain my man?

HAINEAU.
What does it matter? [*Taking his hat and stick and preparing to go.*] Good-bye, you know now what you ought to know. When Hérénien comes down, prepare him to see me.
          [*He goes out. Renewed tempest of howls and cries. HÉRÉNIEN enters.*

CLAIRE. [*Pointing towards the crowd.*]
People must be wicked when the best of them become savage so soon.

HÉRÉNIEN.
Come, have patience. I am as tenacious as the peasant my father. Yesterday, these cries pursued me through the whole house, they beat against the walls from

top to bottom, from cellar to attic, everywhere, like alarm-bells. I felt a rage creeping over me, I would like to have strangled them, stamped them to bits, annihilated them. I was in a fever of hate. I answered their nameless rages with insults. To-day, I feel quite firm. [*Unfolding a letter.*] Listen, this is what has been sent to me: "I can now give you a definite assurance. All the officers are now won over to our cause and will follow us: some out of spite, others out of envy, all out of disgust. We came to an understanding yesterday in a secret meeting. I hold them in my hand. They will obey me like the pen with which I write to you, like the man who carries you this letter. Through them the whole army is ours. The generals? They are too far off, to high; the soldiers are hardly aware of them: they may be overlooked." [*Folding the letter.*] And this letter comes to me from Hordain, the captain of the enemy.

       [*Fresh outbreak of cries: "Death to him!"*
                    "Down with him!"*]

CLAIRE.
My friend!

HÉRÉNIEN.
Well, let them cry on! As for that, I foresaw that the Regency, when it promised anything, when it gave up everything, kept the half up its sleeves, like the jugglers in fairs. It was the maddest thing to go to the Aventine! But I had to have the people, I had to have my people and its fervour, before I could make terms with the besiegers.

CLAIRE.
How reasonable you are now!

THE DAWN

HÉRÉNIEN.
The Regency fooled me perfectly! Those vacuous
and bedizened folk, measuring my ambition by their
own, came here, to offer me a block of its ruined
power: as if men like me did not conquer their own
place, for themselves, in the sight of all. They went
out of that door like beaten lackeys, and since then
my loss has enfuriated them. They have only a few
days more to live, and there is nothing but their rage
for my downfall to keep their thoughts from their
own death-agony. Ah! if the people knew! All the
appearances are against me. I believe in a poor scrap
of writing, a mere signature, scratched out with the
same pen that set it down. The more the Regency
has broken its promises, the more I seem to have
broken mine. Really, they might believe me a
guilty accomplice.

CLAIRE.
It is the people that is. You have only been able to
deceive them because you have been deceived yourself. The innocence of all you have done blinds
them. Ah! I have my own idea. The masses are
as suspicious, as malignant, as ungrateful, as stupid,
as those who govern them. They will never admit
that anyone can be simply pure and great.

HÉRÉNIEN.
I forbid you to think that.

CLAIRE.
You said it yourself yesterday.

HÉRÉNIEN.
Oh! I, that is different. [*Pause.*] The people loves
me, and I love it, despite all, through all. What is
happening now is only a lover's quarrel.
                    [*Insulting shouts in the street.*

THE DAWN

CLAIRE.

They are there by their thousands insulting us. And
those are the same mouths that cheered you! Ah!
the cowards! the wretches! the madmen!

[*Renewed tempest of cries.*

HÉRÉNIEN.

Indeed, one might think they had never known me.

[*Going towards the window with clenched fists.*

Oh! those brutes! those brutes! those brutes!

[*Then, returning to his desk.*

And yet yesterday, at the meeting in the Old Market,
they all cheered me. Haineau defended me with
such fervour that I forgive him all. Le Breux came
to me to-night with the most reassuring news. The
duplicity of the Regents is becoming clearer and
clearer. All Oppidomagne returns to its true master.
My hour has come again. Has it not? [*Impatiently.*]
Has it not, then?

CLAIRE.

There is good hope of it.

HÉRÉNIEN.

No, no, but there is certainty!
Despite these heady cries, despite their multitude,
I can divine already such a flock of hands
All bending to my strength, to me, to-morrow!
My past returns again, and fills their minds,
In a great flood of memories
And in a foam of glory. [*As if speaking to himself.*
I hold the future fast, in these two hands of mine:
Those who withstand,
And those who put their trust in me,
Deep in their conscience know it, all of them.
That noble dream which is made flesh in me,
Now more than ever, spurs me on to live;

THE DAWN

These are the times and these the hours that fire
    my soul.
What are these cries to me, these clamours on the
    wind,
And these unterrifying storms?
Only the future, in my mind,
Far stronger and more real than the present, lives!

CLAIRE. [*Pointing to the street.*]
If they could only see you, how they would be won
by your confidence!
My friend, you make of me
The proudest woman on earth,
And I abase myself and lose myself in your great
    soul;
Take, take this kiss I give to you,
Take it, and bear it where you go,
As a clear shining weapon bear it!
There are few men upon the earth
That ever took
A deeper and a truer one than this!

HÉRÉNIEN.
If my own self were to forsake me, I should find
myself again in you, my force has passed so into your
·heart! But I am so unshaken in my destiny that
nothing which is happening now seems to me real.
I believe in surprise, chance, the unknown. [*Pointing to the street.*] Let them howl on! they are preparing their repentance.
        [*The tumult grows greater. Blows are heard
            on the door below. Window-panes are
            smashed.*

HÉRÉNIEN.
If they go on knocking, I will open.

63

THE DAWN

CLAIRE.
It would be mad.

HÉRÉNIEN.
There have been moments when my mere presence
meant victory! Never have I repelled them, when
they approached my threshold.

> [HÉRÉNIEN *thrusts aside* CLAIRE, *who tries
> to stop him, rushes to the window, opens
> it, and plants himself there with his
> arms folded. The uproar becomes quieter,
> then stops, and there is silence. Sudden-
> ly, at a distance, other cries are heard:
> "Down with the Regency! Down with
> the firebrands! Long live Hérénien!"*]

HÉRÉNIEN.
At last! There is the true people! The people that
cheered me at the Old Market! My heart never
deceived me. It heard when my ears were still deaf.

> [*There is a swaying and jostling in the
> crowd, contradictory outcries, then, slow-
> ly, quietude.*]

CLAIRE. [*At the window.*]
Le Breux is going to speak. Listen.

HÉRÉNIEN. [*Impatiently.*]
I want to speak myself.

LE BREUX. [*In the street.*]
Hérénien was sincere and just. [*Murmurs.*] There
are five hundred of you howling at him, and there is
not one of you whom he has not helped. [*Murmurs.*]
As for me, he extricated me from the very talons of
the consular judges. Last year, he battled to deliver
Haineau. And you, all of you? he saved you in the
time of the tragic and famishing strikes, he . . .

64

THE DAWN

HÉRÉNIEN. [*Impatiently.*]
I have no need of a defender. [*Addressing* LE BREUX, *who speaks in the street.*] I must take the people: I must not have them given to me.

THE CROWD.
—Let him speak.
—Down with him! death to him! He is a traitor!
—Let him speak!
—Death to him! Down with him! He is bought!
—Silence! [*Quiet is restored.*

HAINEAU. [*In the street.*]
I, Charles Haineau, suspected Jacques Hérénien. He seemed to me a man to be doubted. Like you, I opposed him. To-day, I regret it.

THE CROWD. [*Contradictorily.*]
Long live Hérénien! Death to him! Down with him!

HAINEAU.
The Regency sent emissaries amongst us: I surprised them yesterday at the meeting in the Old Market: they were urging other wretches to kill Jacques Hérénien, to pillage his house, to pretend that it was the vengeance of the people.

THE CROWD.
—Death to the Regents!
—Long live the people of Oppidomagne!
—Long live Hérénien!

HAINEAU.
We need Hérénien.

65   F

THE DAWN

THE CROWD.
—Why did he receive dubious messages?
—Why did he leave our meetings?
—He is a despot.
—He is a martyr.
— Let him defend himself.
—Silence!
—May he forgive us!

HÉRÉNIEN.
Forgive you, yes: for a man such as I am is not
doubted; for the Regency of Oppidomagne deceives
as easily as I take breath. Bit by bit, the fine front
of its authority is chipped away; rag by rag the fine
cloak of its power falls from its shoulders. It called
on me to sew together the pieces. It dispatched me
to the Aventine, with the design of monopolizing or
ruining me. The mission was difficult, dangerous,
tempting. I acquitted myself of it as of a duty, and
to-day I am neither lost to you nor gained by it; I
am, and I remain, free; as always, I set my strength
to serve my supreme idea. [*Some cheers.*] Just now
I heard cries of "Bought! Bought!" [*Turning and
seizing a bundle of papers on his desk.*] "Bought!"
What have they not done that I should not be!
[*Brandishing a roll of papers.*] In this handful of
letters they have promised me everything that infamy
can abandon to an apostate, corruption to a traitor.
That you may touch and handle the cynicism, the
policy, the perfidy, the baseness, the blindness of the
Regency, I hand over to you their letters. They
were all accompanied by pressing demands, they
were all the prologue of more ardent solicitations,
all of them contain no more than the shadow of the
infamies that came out in personal interviews. What
they dared not write, they said; what they dared

THE DAWN

not endorse, they impressed; what they dared not
formulate, they hinted. They returned to the attack,
after each failure; they answered refusals by bigger
offers. Finally, they gave up all pride. I needed but
to have opened my hand, to seize the whole power,
and personify, in my own person, all the past. Ah!
truly I wonder at myself when I think with what
violence this fist remained clenched.

And now for the letters, read them yourselves.
[*He throws them to the crowd.*] Talk them over, share
them amongst you, spread them to the four winds
of Oppidomagne. The immense ruin of the Regency
is in them. You will understand all. As for me, I
rest all my security on the insane imprudence of
disarming myself; I am lost, for ever, willingly,
joyously, in the eyes of the Consuls; I offer them
the most unforgettable of insults and I take refuge
in your justice. Henceforth, it is you who protect
my life. [*Cries of enthusiasm.*] I may be attacked,
on any side. Am I not the shining target, at which
all the arrows are aimed?

Swear to me then,—no matter what the calumny
that may be reported, no matter what the fable,
foolish or looking like truth, that may be invented—
swear to follow me, with eyes shut, but with assured
heart. [*They swear, and cheer.*] It should be our
joy and our pride to belong to one another, to hate,
to love, and to think as one. [*Cheers.*] I will be your
soul, and you my arms. And together we shall
realize such splendid conquests of humanity, that
seeing them, thanks to us, living and shining in their
very eyes, men shall date time from the day of our
victory. [*Cheers; then calm; HÉRÉNIEN adds.*] And
now, I request Vincent Le Breux and Charles
Haineau to join me here. I wish no faintest differ-
ence to exist between us. [*Renewed cheers. HÉRÉ-*

THE DAWN

NIEN *turns and goes up to* CLAIRE, *who embraces him.*]
You see now that we should never despair of the
people. [*After a silence.*] Tell our emissary from
Hordain to come here immediately.
            [HAINEAU *and* LE BREUX *enter.* CLAIRE
                        goes out.

LE BREUX.
This is victory!

HAINEAU.
Oh! you are really a master. When I fight against
you I am without force; I am worth a thousand,
when I am by your side.

HÉRÉNIEN.
Well, this time at least, our good old Regency seems
finally stuck in its own mud. [*Sitting down.*] Despite
all its promises and oaths, no help was given to the
household of any of the revolters. It assigned our
men to the most dangerous posts: manipulation of
the powder and explosives. The enemy's bombs fell
into their midst as they worked. Lists of suspected
persons were drawn up: each of the military leaders
had his own.

LE BREUX.
You must regret your action at the Aventine.

HÉRÉNIEN.
Come now! [*Turning sharply to* HAINEAU.] Do you
know, Charles Haineau, what I planned out while
you were urging these storms of revolt against me?

HAINEAU.
Master, believe that all that, my part in it . . .
68

THE DAWN

HÉRÉNIEN.

Do not excuse yourself, do not interrupt; have I not forgotten everything? Yes, over the heads and the thousand arms of this now conquered outbreak, I realized the boldest dream of my life, the one for which alone I exist. [*Rising suddenly.*] In less than three days the enemy will enter Oppidomagne peacefully and we shall welcome them.

HAINEAU.

It is impossible.

HÉRÉNIEN.

The Regent's men have never ceased tempting me. I have discussed patiently with them, questioning, illusioning them, asking for guarantees and confidences; giving them hope and taking it from them in turn, worming out all their secrets; opposing, to their senile tactics, my abruptness and my anger. I played with them audaciously, madly; and I know now, better than anyone, better especially than they themselves, how inevitable and how close is their ruin. Their treasury? Empty. Their munition? Exhausted. Their garners? Ransacked. No more bread for the seige; no more money for the defence. They are asking in what waste, what orgies, fortunes and public supplies have disappeared. Everyone accuses everybody.

The army? The day before yesterday five battalions refused to march. The ringleaders were condemned to death. They were led to the place of execution: not a soldier would fire upon them: they are alive yet. [*Cheers in the street:* " *Long live Hérénien!* "] At the council, the Consuls squabble. Does one propose a plan? His neighbour opposes it, details his own, and wants that to be adopted. A

69

week since, the ministers decided on a general sortie by the Gate of Rome; they succeeded in getting it voted: not a Consul would put himself at the head of the troops.

Each Regent has sent me his emissary: these old men are not even agreed between themselves. They are like poor caged screech-owls, whose perches are turned round. They lose their heads, cry out, and close their eyes against the fire of day. They cast at one another the stupidities, faults, and crimes, for which they are afraid to take the responsibility. "What is to be done?" becomes the motto of their reign.

CLAIRE. [*Entering.*]
The emissary has come.

HÉRÉNIEN.
Let him come in. [*Turning towards* HAINEAU *and* LE BREUX.] I have shown you the situation as it is among us in the city; you shall judge of what it is like among the enemy. Then you will see that war is no longer possible. [*Presenting the emissary to* LE BREUX *and* HAINEAU.] Here is one I am sure of. He knows, more than any of us, as to the state of mind of both armies. [*To the emissary.*] Tell them what you have discovered.
[HÉRÉNIEN *walks to and fro in the room.*

THE EMISSARY.
Last Tuesday night my brother was sent to reconnoitre at the outposts. He went on a long way, to find out if the entrenchment that we had bombarded had given way, and would give us the chance of a general sortie from the Gate of Rome.

THE DAWN

HÉRÉNIEN. [*Interrupting.*]
This is the sortie I told you of.

THE EMISSARY. [*Continuing.*]
All at once, in the dark, a voice calls out, but gently,
as if afraid of frightening him and driving him away.
A few quick, friendly words are exchanged. He is
asked if there are not really in Oppidomagne respon-
sible men who have had enough of the war.

HÉRÉNIEN. [*Quickly.*]
That happened two days ago, and since then there
have been many similar colloquies.

THE EMISSARY.
My brother answers that Oppidomagne will defend
itself, that the revolt against this mutual slaughter
must come, not from the conquered, but from the
conquerors. And other soldiers come up, and say
the besiegers are tired out, that deserters are endless,
that rebellions are breaking out every day, that there
is no longer an army, that they will have to raise
the siege, if the frightful epidemic which decimates
the troops continues. They want the union of all
the miseries against all the powers.

HÉRÉNIEN.
Well, who then, after such an affirmation of human
solidarity, would dare affirm that the conscience of
men remains unchanged?
O these first trembling confidences that come
By night, between the perilous dark
And the terrors of war and its despair;
These first confessions of the true soul of man,
Lucid at last and triumphing,
The passionless stars
On high must rejoice to hear them!

71

THE DAWN

HAINEAU.

Truly, I admire you! At the tiniest glimmer that reaches you through the crack of a door, you are certain of the immense presence of the sun. Since Oppidomagne was blockaded, has a day passed, a single day, without traps being laid for you? Who guarantees you the sincerity of the soldiers? Who tells you that Oppidomagne will open its walls, even to unarmed enemies? You believe everything, like a blind man. The force that animates you is as insensate as it is ardent!

HÉRÉNIEN.

It is the only true one: be in the service of circumstances, hold oneself at the mercy of the immense hope that thrills through the whole world to-day!

HAINEAU.

You believe then that the enemy will abdicate its victory, and accept peace without profit?

HÉRÉNIEN.

You reason without knowledge. The vagabonds and the peasants, who at the beginning of the siege were driven back into the country, and who live, God knows how, between the besiegers and us, have given me tidings day by day. Hordain confirms what they have said, and I have checked everything. The bombardment was bound to cease. The epidemic devours the camp: twenty thousand men are dead; the moats of the entrenchment overflow with corpses. A general was killed yesterday by a soldier, who had suddenly gone mad. The lower ranks league together to destroy the works of the siege: they spike the cannon, they throw balls and powder into the

72

THE DAWN

river. It is thus universal misery, distress, sorrows, tears, rages, terrors, that bring about these hopes of fellowship, these deep and fraternal cries. The very force of things is in accord with ours.

LE BREUX.
You are wonderful. You were thought to be over-come, and now you are preparing for a more gigantic enterprise than ever.

HÉRÉNIEN.
It is because I have faith, a faith capable of com-municating itself to the whole world. I see myself, I feel myself, I multiply myself, in others; I assimi-late them to me. The army of Oppidomagne is in my hands; that of the enemy obeys Hordain, my disciple and my fanatic. We have both worked with enthusiasm. Of what use is ancient wisdom, prudent, systematic, buried in books? It forms part of the humanity of yesterday; mine dates from to-day. [*To the emissary.*] Go and tell those who will be at the outposts this evening that I shall be with them. You will give notice to Hordain.
> [*Cheers in the street. The soldier goes out.*

HÉRÉNIEN. [*To* HAINEAU *and* LE BREUX.]
Will you come with me? Come, tell me quickly.

LE BREUX.
Assuredly.

HÉRÉNIEN. [*To* HAINEAU.]
And you?

73

THE DAWN

HAINEAU.
As long as the leaders live, they may do harm. As long as they have arms, they will kill. They will be the reaction which will follow your victory. Suppress them first.

HÉRÉNIEN.
They will be the past, powerless and annihilated. Come, will you go with me?

HAINEAU.
No.

HÉRÉNIEN.
Good, we will do great things without you.
. [*Renewed cheering in the street.* HÉRÉNIEN *leans out of the window, and is cheered.*

LE BREUX. [*To* HAINEAU.]
He always astonishes me. He sees the obstacle, as you and I do. On what prodigies does he rely to overcome it? And how he carries one along in the whirlwind of his tempest!

HAINEAU.
That man has on his side the unknown forces of life. [*After a pause.*] I shall go with him, after all.

74

THE DAWN

Scene II

*Ruined house. Night, at the outposts. On one side,
rising ground and entrenchments; on the other,
the distant walls of Oppidomagne, faintly lit up.
Le Breux is sitting on a heap of stones; before
him an officer of the enemy, and some soldiers. Silent
groups arrive.*

LE BREUX.
In Oppidomagne, regents, judges, leading men, all
are at the mercy of the people. They are unconscious
of the imminence of their defeat, and imagine that
they still govern. But what Hérénien wishes will
come to pass.

THE OFFICER.
Among us, no one dares punish any more. All the
links that bound us to our leaders and to our kings
have been snapped. We, the inferiors and the poor,
are the masters. To think that after twenty months
of campaigning, after taking six provinces, and ten
strongholds, we should collapse before your disor-
ganized capital!

LE BREUX.
Will Hordain come?

THE OFFICER.
I expect him.

LE BREUX.
I am curious to see him. I do not know him.

75

THE DAWN

THE OFFICER.

He is fifty, he is a mere captain. It was during the
dull and stormy winters of our country of ice, in
the gray and snowy boredom of a little garrison
town, that he won me over to his will and to his
faith. He would sit down, at night, at my chimney
corner, under my lamp; and we would argue. The
works of Hérénien had enlightened him; they were
my light. Hordain explained them to me, commented
on them, with a conviction so profound, that nothing
seemed to me more self-evident in human thought
and justice. Ah! those friendly and ardent evenings
together! You will never know, you people of
Oppidomagne, what miracles can be wrought by a
book on the grave, unsatisfied and profound souls of
a country of shadow and solitude!

> [HORDAIN *and* HÉRÉNIEN *arrive almost at
> the same moment, from opposite direc-
> tions; they are accompanied by officers
> and soldiers.*

HORDAIN.

I come to you, proud to know you. There is not
an idea which we do not share.

HÉRÉNIEN.

I knew by your letters that I could put all my trust
in you. Both of us have our lives at stake, both of
us love one another for the sake of the same profound
and magnificent idea;
And what then if they call us traitors?
Never have we beheld our souls
More proud, more firm, more masters
Of all the future. We stand here,
Hardy and clear, and face to face;
Do we not bring two nations peace?

THE DAWN

Do we not work at good with our rebellious hands?
And conscience cries to us: Well done!

HORDAIN.
Truly, my soul is more peaceful than on a battle-
eve! All the words that justify this understanding
between us have been said centuries ago.

HÉRÉNIEN.
If it were miracles we wanted, they would rise on
every hand. The air we breathe, the horizons we
behold, the fever that beats in our foreheads, the
great burning of which each of us is but a flame,
foretell the new justice.

HORDAIN.
My propaganda was incessant. First, absolutely
secret. Then, the general watchfulness was relaxed
to such a point that my prudence became a mere
luxury. Since the Marshal Hardenz, the only real
leader we had, fell into disgrace, our army exists no
longer. Without understanding anything definite,
our soldiers gather what is in the air. An order! and
they would all go towards Oppidomagne, happy,
confiding, and fraternal. A number of the dead
generals were replaced by captains, of whom some
are ours. It is only the very old leaders who seem to
me impossible to win over. They would be a danger,
if we did not act without delay, sharply, to-morrow.

HAINEAU.
How to-morrow? But time to prepare . . .

HÉRÉNIEN.
We must act like a thunder-clap.

77

THE DAWN

HAINEAU.

But still, it is urgent that Oppidomagne should know
what we want.

HÉRÉNIEN.

She guesses it. To-morrow, she shall know it.

HAINEAU.

But it is impossible to move thousands of men, to
throw open the gates of a city, without taking
measures and assuring ourselves of every chance of
success.

HÉRÉNIEN.

All the measures are taken; all the chances are in
my hand. You alone hesitate and tremble; you
have no faith, you are afraid to believe.

HORDAIN.

This then is what I propose : to-morrow, as soon as
it becomes dark, at seven o'clock, those who are
here and all our friends give orders to their men to
march peacefully towards Oppidomagne. At that
moment, all the leaders who remain to us will be
assembled to feast their first victory. My brother,
with three battalions which are ours, will mount
guard over their debauch. The movement of troops
will start from the east, and go in the direction both
of the gate of Rome and of Babylon: it will reach
them in an hour.

HÉRÉNIEN.

The gate of Rome is too near the Palace and the
Regency. The first part of the troops must enter by
the gate of Babylon, and spread through the quarters
of the people. Ah ! you will see what our people are
like, how they will receive you, cheer for you, breathe

78

into you a stormy and courageous soul. You will pass on your way two barracks, the soldiers of which will join yours; and you will be in the heart of the city while the Regency is still deaf and sleeping.

Only then will you present yourselves at the gate of Rome. The consternation of our masters and their partisans will be in your favour. Only the five hundred consular guards will remain faithful to them. All the other troops lodged in the Palace will receive you with enthusiasm. If there is any fighting between the guards and us, leave our men to settle the affair. Keep out of any sort of quarrel. You need not fire a single shot.

HORDAIN.
We will do scrupulously what you tell us to do.

HÉRÉNIEN.
It is only you, the conquerors, who could realize our dream. Revolutions always begin by the renunciation of a privilege: you renounce victory.

AN OFFICER.
It was only our King who wanted war.

HAINEAU.
Ah, and truly your attack was unjust, your beginning of the campaign . . .

HORDAIN. [*Interrupting.*]
For the last time, let us have things quite clear. My brother will look after the leaders. At eight o'clock three thousand men will enter by the gate of Babylon. Then the gate of Rome opens to let in more battalions. No trumpets, no flags, not a shot fired, no singing. The entry will be sudden, peaceful, and silent. Is that it?

79

THE DAWN

HÉRÉNIEN.

Perfect; we will see to the rest. Oppidomagne is ready; she awaits you. In an hour you will have the whole city yours.

And now, let us separate; do not leave time for objections to come forward, they are weakening, enervating. Our sole tactics shall be: sudden, and bold! Till to-morrow, then, yonder!

> [*They shake hands and separate.* HORDAIN
> *and* HÉRÉNIEN *embrace.*

ACT IV

Scene I

Abode of Hérénien. *Same as in first and second acts.*
The child is playing. Claire *stands anxiously at*
the window.

The Child.
WHAT dress shall I put on Polichinelle?

Claire.
The prettiest.

The Child.
Is it a holiday?

Claire.
The finest holiday of all.

The Child.
Is it Christmas?

Claire.
It is Easter, the real Easter: the first there has ever
been in the world.

The Child.
May I go, if it is a holiday?

THE DAWN

CLAIRE.
It is a holiday for grown-up people; a holiday that children don't understand.

THE CHILD.
Tell me what it is.

CLAIRE.
You will know, one day. You can say then that it is your father, your own father, who made it.

THE CHILD.
Will there be lots of flags?

CLAIRE.
Lots.

THE CHILD.
Then why do you say I should not understand? When there are flags, I always understand.

CLAIRE. [*From the window.*]
At last!
[HÉRÉNIEN *enters with clothes in disorder.*
CLAIRE *rushes towards him.*

HÉRÉNIEN. [*Embracing her feverishly.*]
You know all?

CLAIRE.
I guess, without knowing. Tell me.

HÉRÉNIEN.
Things never happen as one imagines they are going to. I was convinced that none of our chiefs would be at the gate of Babylon: they never are. Yesterday evening, the oldest of them went there. When they saw the enemy at hand, they thought it was an act

82

THE DAWN

of sheer madness. It was not an attack: the order of the troops, the absence of commanders, the lack of organization, proved it. It was not parleyers: there were too many.

When the troops were a hundred yards away, some threw away their arms, others raised the butt ends of their muskets. Without a word, some of our men ran and opened the gates. Our chiefs struggled, shouted, stormed, all together: no one listened to their abuse nor to their orders. All the presentiments they had had, all the fears of defection, of treason, which they dared not admit, must have stabbed and tortured and prostrated them. In a lightning-flash, they understood all. They were surrounded. Three of them were killed: they were brave men. They saw the enemy enter Oppidomagne; they believed it meant defeat, the shame of the last humiliation. Some wept. Our men flung themselves into the arms of the besiegers. There was hand-shaking, embracing. A sudden joy flashed through the souls of all. Swords, knapsacks, cartridges were thrown away. The enemy, whose wine-skins were full, offered drink. And the flood, always bigger and bigger, flows on towards the city and the National Square; our chiefs stand there, pale, mute, incredulous. "It is the end of the war," cried Le Breux in the ear of a commander. "There is neither victory nor defeat: it is holiday." Thereupon the brute began to swear, mad with rage, striking out blindly with his sabre, wounding his horse. Two of his neighbours fled in the midst of the confusion. They went in the direction of the Regency: they will organize perhaps a semblance of resistance, and the consular guard will second them. I have already seen their green uniforms roving about near here.

THE DAWN

CLAIRE.

But the generals of the enemy?

HÉRÉNIEN.

Oh! they are the prisoners of their own army. Yesterday, seeing the troops reduced to half by sickness and desertion, they wanted, in their last despair, to make a great assault. The soldiers refused to advance; some of them fired on their leaders. That ended everything.

CLAIRE.

I have heard the troops pouring into Oppidomagne; it is like the sound of the sea. Never was I at once so happy and so trembling.

HÉRÉNIEN.

Twenty thousand men are now in our midst. Tables are set up in the squares. All those who, during the siege, had hidden away victuals in their cellars, distribute them to the people. Haineau said: "Never will Oppidomagne abase itself to the point of receiving its enemies; never will Oppidomagne permit them to walk about its streets and squares; never will the prejudices of humiliated Oppidomagne be effaced." One reasons in that way in normal times: but to-day!

There is such a confusion in accepted ideas that one could found new religions and proclaim new beliefs. Look, up there, on the heights, the Capitol is in flames! They are burning down the palaces of the Artillery and of the Navy. Before to-night, all the reserves of arms and ammunition will have been served out.

During the siege, justice made for itself banks and exchanges. The hour of doing justice to the

84

THE DAWN

fundamental injustice, war, has come in its turn.
Only with it will the others disappear too: the hate
of the country for the city, of poverty for gold, of
distress for power. The organization of evil has
been struck to the heart. [*Hurrahs are heard in the
street.*] Listen: it is the universal human holiday,
wild and shouting.

> [CLAIRE *and* HÉRÉNIEN *go towards the
> window, and meet in a long embrace.
> All at once* HÉRÉNIEN *disengages him-
> self sharply.*

HÉRÉNIEN.
Dress the child; I came to look for him, so that he
might see my work.

CLAIRE.
The child? But he will not understand.

HÉRÉNIEN.
Dress him all the same; I shall say to him, in the
presence of a world's death, words that he will never
forget. Dress him, that I may take him with me.

CLAIRE.
And I?

HÉRÉNIEN.
Your brother Haineau will come for you.

CLAIRE.
Why can't we all go together?

HÉRÉNIEN.
Dress the child, I tell you, and be quick.

> [CLAIRE *goes out.* HÉRÉNIEN *looks over his
> desk, puts some papers in his pocket,
> then leans from the window, and
> harangues the people.*

THE DAWN

HÉRÉNIEN.
O bitter, shining, and rebellious life
That I have lived and suffered, how it seems
A rest and light and glory to me now!
I feel myself the greater by this conquered world,
Drawn from the depths to light, by these mere
    human hands.
Doubtless it was decreed, a farmer of the plains
Should first be born to give me being, me,
That hugely, with these fingers and these hands of
    mine,
And with these teeth of mine, should grip the throat
    of the law,
And bring to ground the ancient pride of bloody
    powers!
The countryside, from farm to farm, from hut to hut,
Died. In the cities where I came
The universal will
Had fallen on such a depth
Of moral carnage: theft, and lechery, and gold,
Howled at each other and crushed each other,
    thronged
In monstrous hordes of mutual murderous violences.
All the old instincts killed each other, in the narrow
    lists
Of the pot house or the counting-house.
The formidable and accomplice government
Drew for its nourishment and for its bane
The sap of life from those most filthy dunghills,
And swelled with rotten fullness and content.
I was the lightning shining at the window
Where certain stood to watch the portents of the sky;
And, less by any skill or any plans of mine
Than by some unknown wild supremacy of love
For the whole wide world, I know not from my
    very self,

THE DAWN

I burst the bolts that held
The brotherhood of man
In prison-walls.
The old Oppidomagne I have cast under me—
Charters, abuses, favours, dogmas, memories—
And see her now arise, the future city of man,
Forged by the thunderbolt, and wholly mine,
Who gaze and see the fire of my immortal thought
And my unconquered folly and ardour realized
Shine and become the light in the fixed eyes of fate!
                              [*Shots are heard.*

CLAIRE. [*From her room.*]
Hérénien, the Regent's soldiers are coming into the
street.

HÉRÉNIEN. [*Not hearing, continues.*]
I have made the world again in my own image,
I have lifted up the people and their fruitful powers
Out of the night of instinct to the vast
And clear and radiant threshold of my pride.

CLAIRE. [*Re-entering.*]
Hérénien! Hérénien! Armed men are watching the
house. They will kill you, if you go out.

HÉRÉNIEN.
Come, come! Dress the child.   [*Renewed firing.*

CLAIRE.
The shots are coming nearer to the square.

HÉRÉNIEN.
Dress the child.

CLAIRE.
They are spying on you; they are waiting for you;
they want to take your life. . . .

87

THE DAWN

HÉRÉNIEN.
Dress the child.
> [*She goes to fetch the child, who trembles,*
> *takes it in her arms, and protects it.*

CLAIRE.
My friend, I beg of you, do not venture out; wait
till they have passed.

HÉRÉNIEN.
I have no time to wait. To-day I have no fear,
either of others or of myself. I have risen to that
point of human strength.

CLAIRE.
Go then by yourself, and leave me the child.

HÉRÉNIEN. [*With violence.*]
I want the child. I want him there, by my side.

CLAIRE.
He shall come soon. Haineau will bring him to you.

HÉRÉNIEN.
He must be cheered with his father. Give him to
me, come, give him to me.

CLAIRE.
I have never resisted you. I obey you always, like a
slave, but to-day, I entreat you. . . .

HÉRÉNIEN.
Give him to me, I tell you.
> [*He tears the child from the arms of* CLAIRE,
> *thrusts her back, and rushes out with*
> *him.*

88

THE DAWN

CLAIRE.
My friend! my friend! Oh! that madness! Always his poor, colossal madness! [*An immediate sound of firing arrests her. After a moment of frantic anguish, she runs to the window, and leans out, crying.*] My son! my son!

> [*Then she rushes into the street. Noise of horses galloping away. Tumult. Clamours. A silence. Then, dominating all the others:*

A VOICE.
Jacques Hérénien is assassinated!

SCENE II

Morning. The Place of the People, laid out entirely in terraces. In the background is seen the panorama of Oppidomagne, veiled in the smoke of conflagration. To the right the statue of the Regency, in full view, on a platform. To the left the Palace of War is burning. Townspeople deck the windows with flags; drunken men pass. Wild dances cross the scene; bands succeed bands. Songs are heard on all sides. Boys throw stones at the statue of the Regency.

A BEGGAR.
Now then, ragamuffins, look out, you'll have your ears pulled.

THE BOYS.
—We are throwing stones at the Regency, because it's dead.

89

THE DAWN

—[*Throwing a stone.*] Here goes for the sceptre.
—Here goes for the crown.

BANDS. [*Surrounding the statue and singing catches.*]
And count by four and count by three:
And men of mettle, who are they?
They who reject the soldier's pay,
To wrest their rights wherever wrongs may be,
And win their way to liberty.

And count by three and count by two:
The men of mettle, who are they?
They are the men whose hearts are gay
When cities of gold and fire and fever brew
The cup of the wrath of God for you.

And count by two and count by one:
The men of mettle, who are they?
They who with one hand's hammer bray
To dust the dusty hopes and powers that shun
The light of their chief, the light of the sun.

A PEASANT.
Hang me if I ever thought to see Oppidomagne
again!

GROUP OF BEGGARS.
—I hid myself in a hole, like a beast.
—I took turns in serving both parties. The Oppi-
domagne people called me the mole: I let them into
all the projects of the enemy; and the enemy
thought me as subtle as smoke: I kept them posted
in the goings on at Oppidomagne.
—We did the same. I worked north.
—And I, west.
—By betraying the both of them, we have ended

by settling their differences. [*Ironically.*] We have
made peace.

A GIPSY.
Isn't there always a moment when what is called
crime becomes virtue?

A BEGGAR.
Is it true Hérénien is dead?

THE GIPSY.
He! he is master and king now. People don't die
when they are so great as that.

A BEGGAR.
They killed him at his very door.

THE GIPSY.
Who did?

A BEGGAR.
The Consulars.

THE GIPSY.
Impossible!

A BEGGAR.
They might well wish him ill! Never man accomplished so great a work.

THE GIPSY.
It is not a man, it is all of us who have done it.

THE SHEPHERD.
At last we shall be able to find a living!

THE DAWN

THE GIPSY.
We! Come now! the soil of humanity would have
to be quite differently turned up if the light is to
come into our holes and corners. Peace or war,
Still we remain unchanging misery,
Nothing avails to us the idle come and go
Of sorrow or of joy.
Though with new laws Oppidomagne
Should this day set its bitted, bridled people free,
We only shall remain, God only knows till when,
The birds of prey, the wandering birds,
That, little piece by piece, tear up the greedy earth,
Like crows that rich men frighten from their homes,
Chasing them from their thresholds and their or-
        chard-plots,
Although they give free welcome there
To the whole race of birds as free.

THE SHEPHERD.
You speak as if the Regency still lived. The country
will be reborn. The cities are purging themselves.

THE GIPSY.
Fortunately! everything is only a going towards
something, and to-morrow will always be dissatisfied
with to-day. [*A troop of drunken women crosses the
scene, with torches. They shout: "To the churches!
to the churches! Burn down God!" To the beggar.*]
Look at those, there are your allies! When you and
your friends have decided to be really men, come
and look for me, as others went and found Hérénien.
                    [*He goes away.*

GROUP OF WORKMEN. [*Putting up a platform on
        which to lay the corpse of* HÉRÉNIEN. *They
        bring the black cloth.*
—This is a bad business if there ever was one.

92

THE DAWN

—He had two shots there, in the forehead.

—Was his son killed?

—No.

—Nobody knows which of the guards were the assassins. They got away. Perhaps we shall never know the name of the abominable coward who killed our tribune.

—There was fighting, outside the Regency. It took an hour to dislodge the consulars. Hérénien was already dead.

A BEGGAR.

They say Haineau killed him.

A WORKMAN.

Haineau? You don't know what you are talking about! Haineau! why he is more distressed about it than we are.

A BEGGAR.

He was his enemy.

THE WORKMAN.

Be silent; you lie by all the teeth in your jaws.

THE BEGGAR.

I say what I was told.

THE WORKMAN.

It is people like you who start all the foul stories.

[*Enemies and soldiers of Oppidomagne pass along arm in arm, and crowd on the terrace and steps.*

THE CROWD.

—Will the holiday come off?

93

THE DAWN

—Why not? It is the new leaders of Oppidomagne who ordered it.

—Never did Hérénien seem so great as in his death.

GROUP OF PASSERS.

—They carry him through the whole city in triumph.

—I saw him crossing the Marble Square. There was a red wound across his face.

—And I, I saw him pass the Haven Bridge;
Mothers with lifted arms
Held out their little ones to him,
So that all young and joyous things
That life can offer to a man
Hovered and bent above this man in death.

—He passes, garlanded with dedicated flowers;
The scarlet shroud enfolds him in a light of flames;
His body:
A very storm of love, like waves of the sea,
Billows him high and holds him over all men's
        heads;
Never did king, shining with gold,
With blood, with murder, and with battles,
Have at his death
So glorious and so kingly great a funeral.

—At the Colonnades a young man made his way up to the litter. He dipped his handkerchief in the blood on the cheeks, and long and fervently, as if he received the host, he put it to his lips.

A WORKMAN. [*Who has heard them talking.*]
Jacques Hérénien will be laid out here, on this platform, here, in our midst, in all his glory.

A PEASANT.
It is good for the sun to see him.

94

THE DAWN

—Tears, flowers, songs, blood, dances, fire: all conflicting ardours burn in the air!
—It is the right atmosphere when new worlds are created.

> [*An immense influx;* LE BREUX, *followed by soldiers and workmen, goes upon the step before a house and makes signs that he wishes to speak. Silence.*

LE BREUX.
Citizens, in a few moments you will see in this square of Oppidomagne, dedicated to the people, the body of Jacques Hérénien. Receive him as a conqueror. A few shots have been enough to close his eyes, stiffen his arms, immobilize his face, but not to kill him. Jacques Hérénien lives still, in his words, in his acts, in his thought, in his books; he is the force which now exalts us; he wills, thinks, hopes, acts in us. This is not his burial, it is his last victory. Stand back: he comes.

> [*Children climb up on people's shoulders. Enormous anxiety in all groups. People get on the windows, climb columns.*

DIFFERENT GROUPS ON THE TERRACES.
—What a crowd! The square will never hold them!
—How they loved him! People like that ought never to die.

GROUP OF WOMEN.
—His wife follows the bier.
—It is she who is carrying the child.
—She is a Christian!
—A Roman!

95

THE DAWN

—Silence : here is the body.

[*The bier comes forward, and is borne round*
the square; some weep, others cheer,
others fall on their knees, some women
make the sign of the cross. On the
terraces, clusters of people squeeze to-
gether to see better.

YOUNG MEN. [*Marching before the body. With*
prayer and exultation.]
—Hérénien, Hérénien, you were our only master !
—There is not any spark of all my thought
You fanned not with your ardour, like a mighty
    wind.

—Hérénien, Hérénien, 'tis you survive in us !
We vow and dedicate to you
All that our souls one day
Shall fashion us of beauty and of strength and light
And purity in life !

—Hérénien, Hérénien, your memory
Shall be the pulse and heart-beat of the times to-
    come !

—Hérénien, Hérénien, enliven us
That we be always thus, these mad and vehement
    ones,
That, in ill times,
Now past, your impulse hurried
Out of our weak and wandering ways
Into the whirlwind of your might !

[*The corpse is set down on the platform;*
women cover the black cloth with
flowers.

THE DAWN

THE SEER. [*Standing on one of the terraces above the crowd.*]
What hour is near?
Sounds, not of tears, I hear.
This is indeed the hour
When, fatal to the gods, thunder has rolled
To cast them down, haggard and old,
Since sudden truth shines out, in vindicating power!

The hope of man is now again made flesh;
The old desire, replenished with new flowers, new
    youth,
Springs from the earth; now eyes have light and
    hearts have truth,
And these magnetic rays bind soul to soul afresh.

And now with shining palms veil over and hide deep
This mortuary crape that covers one asleep;
And now beware lest you profane
The worship and the fame
Of so pure, powerful, and divine a name,
Or this dead man has died in vain.

He was in harmony with the new birth
That waits the world, and with the stars, and time;
He has won life through mortal tumult, mortal crime;
He has crushed under him one of the plagues of earth!
        [HORDAIN *rises in agitation. The crowd*
             point to him and cheer. People tell one
             another who he is.

THE CROWD.
—It was he who refused to attack Oppidomagne.
—He won over the enemy.
—He is as great as Hérénien.

THE DAWN

HORDAIN. [*Pointing to the corpse.*]
I was his disciple, and his unknown friend. His books were my Bible. It is men like this who give birth to men like me, humble, faithful, long obscure, but whom fortune permits, in one overwhelming hour, to realize the supreme dream of their master. If fatherlands are fair, sweet to the heart, dear to the memory, armed nations on the frontiers are tragic and deadly; and the whole world is yet bristling with nations. It is in their teeth that we give them this example of our concord. [*Cheers.*] They will understand some day the immortal thing accomplished here, in this illustrious Oppidomagne, whence the loftiest ideas of humanity have taken flight, one after another, through all the ages. For the first time since the beginning of power, since brains have reckoned time, two races, one renouncing its victory, the other its humbled pride, are made one in an embrace. The whole earth must needs have quivered, all the blood, all the sap of the earth must have flowed to the heart of things. Concord and goodwill have conquered hate. [*Cheers.*] Human strife, in its form of bloodshed, has been gainsaid. A new beacon shines on the horizon of future storms. Its steady rays shall dazzle all eyes, haunt all brains, magnetize all desires. Needs must we, after all these trials and sorrows, come at last into port, to whose entrance it points the way, and where it gilds the tranquil masts and vessels. [*Enthusiasm of all: the people shout and embrace. The former enemies rise and surround* HORDAIN. *Those of Oppidomagne stretch their arms towards him. He disengages himself from them and lays palms at the feet of* HÉRÉNIEN. *Then turning towards the widow.*] In the name of life and the triumph of life, I demand of you, Claire Hérénien, to present to these two exultant people, him who

98

THE DAWN

seems to us to be Jacques Hérénien himself: his
son!   [*He holds out his arms to present the child.*

CLAIRE. [*Staying him.*]
I want to have strength to do it myself. [*She rises.*]
Here, in the city's very heart,
Here, at this moment great with hope,
Upon this threshold of new days, that bring
A new beginning to the world;
Drying my tears, and calling on my will,
I dare confide to you this child, child of his flesh,
I dare devote this child to proud, to tragic duty,
To that chimaera, dazzling and divine,
His father bridled and broke in and rode.
I offer him to the future, jubilant in this place
Of feast and insurrection aureoled,
Here in this place of joy and sorrow, even here
Before you all, before the feet of this slain man
Who was Hérénien, and is dead!
                [CLAIRE *holds up the child in her arms for*
                some time in the midst of cheers and
                waving of arms, then passes him to
                HORDAIN, *and, unable to control her-*
                self any longer, falls sobbing on the
                corpse. Silence comes slowly.

LE BREUX.
This hour is too great and too beautiful, it binds us
too intimately to each other, for us to think of oaths
or terms of peace. In full liberty, in face of all that
remains, inviolate and sacred, in face of this man of
genius, whose murdered body and immortal soul
enfever and inspire us, we give ourselves, each to
each, for ever!   [*Cheers.*

HORDAIN.
Yesterday, when with open hands and hearts we
                        99

entered the city, I was amazed that he who more than all of us had realized our work should be present, in life, at his triumph. So great a conquest required so great a victim. If you consider under what strange circumstances Hérénien, without escort, without arms, offered himself to perhaps the last shot that was fired, you will believe, as I do, that his death is bound up in the mystery of the great and sovereign powers.

HAINEAU.
He broke under him the old power whose image still stands upright. [*He points to the statue; there are cries: " Pull it down! Pull it down!" Workmen seize crowbars to pull it down, and mount the pedestal.*] He conquered its spawn, its dastard consuls, its bastard laws, its shameful customs, its paid armies.

THE CROWD.
Pull it down! Pull it down!

HAINEAU.
He purged its thieving banks, its treasury, its parliaments and its councils: he slew all antagonisms. That image mocks his action.
[*He points to the statue.*

THE CROWD.
—Oh! the old brute!
—Luckless doll!
—Horrible drab!

ON ALL SIDES.
Pull it down! Pull it down!

THE CROWD.
—Throw it into the sewers!

THE DAWN

—Break it! Smash it to pieces!
—Pull it down! Pull it down!

SOMEONE FROM THE FIELDS.
It was that that devoured us!

SOMEONE FROM THE CITIES.
It was that that blighted us!

SOMEONE FROM THE FIELDS.
It was death!

SOMEONE FROM THE CITIES.
It was crime!

ON ALL SIDES.
Pull it down! Pull it down!

A WORKMAN. [*From the pedestal, to those around.*]
Look out: it is going to fall, it is going to fall!
> [*In the midst of outcries of hate the huge
> statue totters and falls. There is im-
> mediate silence. Then* HAINEAU *seizes
> the head, which remains intact, and,
> staggering under its colossal weight,
> flings it and breaks it, without a word,
> at the feet of* HÉRÉNIEN.]

THE SEER.
Now let the Dawn arise!

THE CLOISTER

A PLAY IN FOUR ACTS

TRANSLATED BY
OSMAN EDWARDS

PREFACE

POETRY and drama, once intimately allied, have been so little associated of late years that a dramatist who casts his story in poetic form must usually look for appreciation to a staunch minority. To such a minority Emile Verhaeren, in his dramas at least, has hitherto addressed himself, shaping his vision in accordance with independent standards, and confidently awaiting the verdict of more fastidious taste than is fostered in the "commercial theatre." Naturally, therefore, the success of *Le Cloître* has been a striking but gradual *succès d'estime*, enhanced by fine acting and enthusiastic criticism in those cities—Brussels, Paris, Berlin, Moscow, Manchester, and latterly, London—where special audiences are willing to welcome plays of special calibre. It is hoped that the present version, made in close collaboration with the author some fourteen years ago, and following with fidelity his alternations of elaborate lyric and staccato prose, will convey a fair suggestion of those unconveyable qualities which make the original unique.

Le Cloître was written in 1899 and published in 1900. M. Reding produced it in the latter year at the Théâtre Royal du Parc of Brussels, where it ran for a fortnight and has been often revived. At

PREFACE

Paris M. Lugné-Poe offered it the hospitality of the Théâtre de l'Œuvre. Ten years later Berlin and Manchester followed suit. It may be surmised that in neither city was a Protestant audience likely to grasp the full significance of such a play. Journals commended it to attention as being "a Play without a Woman." To ask the playgoer to forgo sexual interest betrayed an abnormal playwright. It is well to remember, therefore, that for the author and for Belgium at the end of last century Catholicism in education, politics, art, and every other form of activity was a fact of dominant importance. Brought up in an orthodox atmosphere, the young poet derived his clearest impressions of the cloister from a retreat of three weeks spent in a monastery near Chimay. The result was a slim volume of poems— *les Moines*—which are sometimes said to contain the germs of the play written thirteen years afterwards. But they are little more than water-colour sketches of monastic experience in comparison with the solidly drawn figures and careful composition of the ultimate picture. The play has a charm, which is more than pictorial, as the poems are—more even than dramatic. Not only does it unfold a tragic story of human misery intensified by a religious setting, but interwoven with the conflict between a man and destiny is a more shadowy but equally real conflict between ideas. Behind each monk, behind Balthazar, Thomas, Mark, the Prior, stands an idea, one of the weapons with which the Church has conquered the world. Behind the whole group of

106

monks is an ecclesiastical ideal, that of separate and exclusive jurisdiction, one that seemed no less injurious to the community in the author's eyes than the military claim to a similar privilege, which, at the time of the composition of the play, was causing the case of Dreyfus to ring through Europe. The presence of these large but implicit rather than explicit factors in the problem of Balthazar's ruin must be borne in mind, if we would realize the scope of the poet's aim. Superficially we are concerned with the struggle for succession to the Priorate between two rivals, of whom the loser is disqualified by suicidal remorse. Actually, however, Balthazar is not merely the victim of a frantic conscience. He is also the spokesman of emotional, intuitive faith, which contrasts with the keen and subtle scholasticism of his opponent. How contemptuously does the Prior's ancestral pride dismiss the childlike simplicity of Mark! The sympathetic insight with which such various types are drawn and the skill with which their interaction is utilized to entangle the soul of the parricide, have the effect of deepening our interest in the issue. We seem to witness not merely the ordeal of a monk, but also the trial of a monastery, before the tribunal of modern thought. Not as an advocate, but as an artist Verhaeren presents the case, draping each participant in turn with folds of splendid rhetoric.

Such reflections are more likely to occur to a reader than to a spectator, for in the theatre one is, or should be, enthralled by the art of the actor. Of

PREFACE

the five Balthazars whom I have seen the most fiery, the most tragic was certainly M. de Max. The performance given by M. Liten's company at the Kingsway Theatre in January 1915, would have been more convincing if the part of Dom Mark had not been left in feminine hands. Apart from this the *ensemble* was excellent. Gratitude no less than honesty impels me to record that no foreign impersonator of the gentle boy-monk was able to express the beauty and tenderness of the part so perfectly as Mr. Esmé Percy, who induced Miss Horniman to mount *The Cloister* for a week at the Gaiety Theatre, Manchester, on 3 October 1910. There was no wave of pro-Belgian sympathy at that time to float the play into fame, but the critics declared its production to be "a triumph of courage and initiative." Its reception by both press and public on its own merits, aided, of course, by a competent and well-trained company, encourages me to believe that the "translator" is not wholly "traitor." Mr. Percy has undertaken to introduce the play during the coming season to the people of Birmingham, Newcastle, Glasgow, and Edinburgh. His long and intimate acquaintance with this drama, which dates from its first performance in Brussels, should ensure for it a faithful and fervent lease of life among lovers of great poetry, even though it be seen through the glass, darkly, of Anglo-Saxon translator and interpreters.

OSMAN EDWARDS.

PERSONS OF THE DRAMA

Dom Balthazar.
Dom Mark.
The Prior.
Father Thomas.
Dom Militien.
Idesbald.
Theodule.
Monks.

THE CLOISTER

ACT I

A convent garden with symmetrical flower-beds, box-hedges, arbours, and sun-dial; to the right towards the front, a Calvary; to the left, Roman archway, leading to the chapel; at the back, MONKS *are playing bowls, working at fishing-nets, and mending garden-tools. Some, seated in a circle on a broad wooden bench, are engaged in discussion.*

THOMAS. [C.]
I WAS saying then: God cannot be evil. Now, if we only fear that which is evil, why is it taught that "The *fear* of God is the beginning of wisdom?"

BALTHAZAR. [*Walks up and down impatiently.*]
You are too fond of argument.

THOMAS.
The matter is important. If you decide this question wrongly, you put the whole life of a Christian on a false basis.

BALTHAZAR.
You are too fond of argument, I tell you.

MARK. [*Extreme* R.]
We should not fear God; we should love Him.

THE CLOISTER

THOMAS.
You talk like the arch-heretic, Basilides.

MARK. [*Advancing.*]
I? Like Basilides?

THOMAS.
Basilides says in so many words what you affirm.

MARK.
Saint Augustine says it, too.

MILITIEN.
Dom Mark is right. Saint Augustine does say in so
many words, " *Love and do what thou wilt.*"

THOMAS.
Oh! that is not at all the same thing. Saint Augustine reserves fear. The worshipper should vary his
adoration; he should be at once both fearful and
trembling and full of fervour. . . .

BALTHAZAR. [*Impatient.*]
You are too fond of argument, too fond of argument. . . .

THOMAS. [*To* BALTHAZAR.]
My brother, you do not distinguish the infinite
diversity of the Divine Nature and Personality.

BALTHAZAR. [*Abruptly. Advances to* c.]
A passion, a rage for God is what I feel;
I hear but one appeal,—
Theirs, who proclaim
With all but frantic eulogy His Name;
As if they found no language but a cry,

THE CLOISTER

One cry, their mad life long,
But clear as lustral water, pure and strong. [*A pause.*
God does not ask to be described, to be
Weighed and dealt out in volumes grandiose
Pompous with solemn pride.

THOMAS.
Thy faith grows simply, as grass grows,
Contented on God's threshold to abide;
But God to-day, when Thought stirs every mind,
Must be discussed, that He may win mankind.

BALTHAZAR. [*Violently.*]
He is most God, when comprehended least.
When faith and love for weariness have ceased
To hold Christ up—bare—bleeding—before men,
Then man seeks to explain Him, it is then
Man wastes his hour in vain, deep argument.
How God must laugh to see such reason spent
On spiteful and vainglorious exercise!
He loathes this vulgar trade of "Hows" and "Whys"
Wherein His Name stands quoted, high or low,
As the defender's skill plead well or no.
God is more high than human sages dream;
He is too vast, too deep, too infinite
For man to sound His depth, or scale His height;
And only in some ecstasy apart
Of loving sacrifice and joy supreme
A Saint has, once or twice, attained His heart!

MILITIEN.
That is the truth!

MARK. [*Full of enthusiasm, advancing towards* BAL-
    THAZAR *and remaining near him.*]
Oh! my brother! my brother!

THE CLOISTER

THOMAS. [*Feigning surprise.*]
We deserve, no doubt, to be flouted and denied.
> [*Addressing the other* MONKS, *who interrupt
> their games to listen without taking part.*

And that is where we stand, we—the successors of
Bonaventura, of Saint Thomas Aquinas!
> [*Addressing* DOM MARK *and* DOM MILI-
> TIEN.

Yet these were Saints! no less than those you claim.
Saints! on whose brows the apostolic flame
Shone like a sword of God with ray serene;
Their hearts in darkling thought had caught the keen,
Essential spark, from which the soul takes fire;
Their faith took reason for a cloth of gold,
And broidered there great lilies fair,
Doctrines sublime and bold,—
Leaving to feebler hearts the dull desire
Of customary prayer.
> [*Taking* BALTHAZAR *directly to task.*

Ay: those were saints indeed! and sages, too,
And heroes, whereas you . . .

BALTHAZAR. [*Troubled.*]
                              Look not on me,
When you are speaking of such men sublime.

MILITIEN.
Greatness has fallen from the heights; our time
Is atheist. It denies the fervent praise,
Which hailed in western lands in ancient days
The hero's purity, the Christian's strength;
When faith fell, shadowing our shores, at length
Came Science and sang her own Magnificat;
Now Science in her turn is pointed at,
A murderess, a destroyer; those deny,

THE CLOISTER

Who dreamed her mistress of bright harmony,
So fair, that she alone explained the world!
Her truth becomes untruth; to-day is hurled
On yesterday; no system is so wide,
But premiss by result is falsified;
Prodigal guesswork spreads and spreads no light;
There is no more false or true, no wrong or right;
Science is dying . . . by herself devoured.

THOMAS. [*Advancing towards* MILITIEN.]
'Tis false! With all the future is she dowered!

MILITIEN.
We must return to the old, simple creed
Of children; love and gentleness we need
And ignorance. I know no man alive,
Whose life will suit the time, when these revive,
Save one, save only Mark here.

BALTHAZAR.   Him I call
Our Highest!

MARK. [*In confusion.*]
                    I? Not I? Among you all
I am the least, the lowliest.

BALTHAZAR.   Thou art the same
As Francis of Assisi, child, whose name
Perfumes and crowns with lilies all the Church.
Oh! beside thee, I feel what black sins smirch,
What heavy sins oppress me. But thou art
Fair innocence, our temple's holiest heart,
Our paragon, a vessel of pure flame.
And were we as those men of fiery fame

Whose ardour turned the Middle Age to gold,
We monks should kiss thy rough robe's hem, should
    hold
Sacred thy tranquil and miraculous hands . . .

MARK. [*Greatly moved.*]
Oh! Balthazar! my brother Balthazar!

BALTHAZAR. [*Violently.*]
I am nothing but a wind, blown fierce and far,
A torch, tossed madly in the tempest's night,
When I behold that fixed and tranquil light,
Which through thy soul unconscious shows so plain!
My pride seems then a thing abject and vain,
When thou art near; I long to mortify
My heart, my flesh, my being; let them lie
Here in the dust below thy shining feet . . .
              [*He falls on his knees, as if insane.*

MARK. [*Tries to lift him.*]
My brother, my poor brother Balthazar! . . .

BALTHAZAR.
Let be; let the mud mar
My fallen falsity of painted pride;
Sin, upon shame and fear, has crucified
My soul, which, wert thou pitiless, would die.

MARK.
O kneel not, Balthazar, I charge thee by
The love that keeps us one: look at me now!
Am I not still thy ward, my guardian thou?

BALTHAZAR. [*Rising.*]
I wished to show myself, compared with thee,
Humble and worthless.

THE CLOISTER

MILITIEN.   Brother, thou hast set
Such high example of frank worthiness,
As fires our fervour.

BALTHAZAR. [*To* MILITIEN.]
                    Pity my distress.

MILITIEN.
Our prayers will not forget . . .

BALTHAZAR. [*To all, going with trembling steps to* R.
    behind columns.]
I bid you all immensely pity me . . .
                    [*He moves away, leaving the* MONKS *aston-
                    ished. Soon* DOM MILITIEN *and* DOM
                    MARK *rejoin him in the arbour. They
                    disappear.*

THOMAS. [*To the* MONKS *who continue absorbed, each
    in his work.*]
Strange—is it not? Suddenly, like a gust of wind, to
fall into such excess of passion! You talk and reason
and prove,—when all at once this astonishing Balthazar breaks all bounds and provokes a sort of
edifying scandal.

IDESBALD.
He is masterful and arrogant; impetuous and wild.
You would fancy him above us all, and look at him
now—more humble, more submissive than the lowest
of lay-brothers.   No one sees his true character.

THOMAS. [*Rises scornfully.*]
You think so?
                    117

THE CLOISTER

IDESBALD.
The security of these cloisters will be gone, if ever
this monk becomes our chief.

THOMAS.
Who would prevent him?

IDESBALD. [*Earnestly.*]
I appeal to every monk here.

THOMAS. [*Mockingly.*]
Oh! They have neither his strength nor his stature.
In his presence they are mute like conquered men.

A MONK.
Because the time to act is not yet come.

THOMAS.
Why, it was always time to act, since first he came!
Our Prior supports Balthazar, because he is Duke
and Count like himself, like Dom Mark and Dom
Militien. His wrinkled hands are always pushing
him in front of us. For ten years I have seen it,
struggled against it, worked against it. To-day,
when I should welcome the help of you all, not one
will move.

A MONK.
We will never accept Balthazar.

THOMAS.
Then defend yourselves. Something tells me, we
must rely on action. . . .

IDESBALD.
Rome will never impose him upon us.

THE CLOISTER

THOMAS.
Dom Balthazar comes of a noble line;
His virtues through his titles doubly shine;
He is rich in sureties and ancestral fame;
For long since came
His ancestor,
Bristling with gold and pillage,
Back to his village,
And dowered with all his store
These cloisters; where we magnify Christ's name.

A MONK.
'Tis an old fable.

THOMAS.
If men think it true, that is enough.

IDESBALD. [*Dreamily.*]
We others are mere clerks and commoners!
Balthazar is Comte d'Argonne, Duc de Rispaire. . . .

THOMAS.
Who least among us all
Is armed with power to foresee,
With living, battling Science? Surely he!
Beyond our narrow monastery-wall
He never notes the lightning, when it sears
With distant flash the enormous, thundering sky;
Of that loud-leaping fight he nothing hears,
Which even God mistrusts uneasily.
His world is bounded by a convent-wall,
To-day, when all creation rings so loud
With deep revolt, by day and night avowed,
That not to hear is not to exist at all,
Or else to be of stone! He only strives
To keep intact the old ascetic dream,

T H E   C L O I S T E R

Dreamed by his forefathers, to reign supreme
Above us all: thus would he cramp our lives.
He comes to us three centuries in arrear!
His soul is harsh, fanatical, austere;
His knowledge is of texts alone; yet he,
Because he acts the Prior, our Prior will be.

A MONK.
'Tis you, who should be Prior.

THOMAS.
That depends on yourselves. You are the new
force, unknown till now, which must assert itself.
Warn the Pope.   Appeal to Rome.

IDESBALD. [*Hesitating.*]
They should nominate you.

THOMAS. [*Looking hard at* IDESBALD.]
And you? What of you?

IDESBALD. [*Feigning indifference.*]
Oh! I? I?

THOMAS. [*Firmly.*]
The sole decision rests with Rome.   The Bishop
favours me.   He detests our Prior.   He will act
outside the monastery, cautiously, with proper regard for precedent.   But you others, for God's sake,
bestir yourselves.

A MONK.
You will tell us what to do.

THOMAS.
Use your own wits.   You must oppose Balthazar
with your words, your attitude, and your aims,

120

whether expressed or not expressed. Oppose him
in every step you take, in every letter you write.
You must ruin him in the eyes of the Prior. You
must shake him in his own eyes, that he may lose
confidence in himself. How can I tell? You must
tell yourselves what to do. . . .

IDESBALD.
Balthazar never seemed so dangerous as to-day.

THOMAS. [*To* IDESBALD.]
He is passing through a crisis of conscience.

THEODULE. [*To the* MONKS.]
Each of us will pray for him.

THOMAS. [*To* THEODULE.]
You will pray for him, when the monastery is safe.

THEODULE. [*Defiantly.*]
Dom Balthazar sets us an example.

THOMAS.
God rises again in spirit, every century, as once His
Body rose again. Each spiritual Resurrection pro-
duces new witnesses to His glory. To-day we are
those witnesses.

THEODULE.
And the Prior? And Dom Mark? And Dom
Militien?

THOMAS.
You understand nothing of the common end, which
we are all anxious to attain. You are like a withered
branch on that tree of life, which God planted long
ago, and still cherishes in this monastery.

THE CLOISTER

THEODULE.
Our duty is to obey.

THOMAS.
We are the majority; we have knowledge and right on our side.   You will see clearly one day.

IDESBALD.
Leave it to us.

A MONK.
You only substitute one ambition for another.

ANOTHER MONK. [*To* IDESBALD *and* THOMAS.]
Balthazar unites you against himself.   If he fell, you would fight one another for his place.

THOMAS. [*To the* MONKS.]
We wish to set you free from the old bondage; we wish to awaken in you more life and power.   Do not be your own enemies.
> [*Silence falls, as the* PRIOR *is seen advancing.*

IDESBALD. [*In a whisper.*]
Leave it to us. . . . Leave it to us. . . .
> [*The old* PRIOR, *leaning on his staff, slowly advances.* THOMAS *goes forward hastily to meet him. The other* MONKS *gradually withdraw and end by disappearing.*

THOMAS. [*To the* PRIOR.]
My father, I have finished my commentaries on Tertullian.   May I send them to his lordship, the Bishop, and ask for his *approbatur*?

122

THE CLOISTER

PRIOR. [*Crosses to* L. *and turns.*]
Monseigneur hopes great things from you.
He admires you, Father Thomas.

THOMAS.
Monseigneur is indulgent.

PRIOR.
You think that I am slower to admire?

THOMAS.
Your patronage is what I most desire.

PRIOR.
You bear a burning torch before God's face,
You pierce the gloom of infinite space
With tracks of fire;
Without such men as you to lead it right
The age would flounder in pitfall and quagmire.
We need pure brows, illumined with the light
Of Science, to subserve eternal Truth,
Just as we need strong hands
To issue firm commands,
Men of imposing race, who, from their youth,
Are wont to dominate large tracts of time.

THOMAS. [*After a pause.*]
With all respect, I hold not less sublime
The strength of those, whom Science has endowed
With ampler minds to dominate the crowd;
They, too, are able, they . . .

PRIOR.
All those, whose eyes see human nature plain,
Have thought as they still think to-day;
Their thoughts agree not with thy thoughts, but
    mine.

I rule: I think: *You* think as I ordain.   [*A pause.*
Hear me: so long as earth shall nourish still
Proud families of immemorial will,
Your hope will rest unrealized.
Their force and strength,
By God alone and not by destiny devised,
Have grown, at length,
So concentrated in such copious store
That they are charged with power for evermore:
To live for them is nothing but to reign.
Wherefore, unless this vast authority,
Grafted from sire to son,
Be flouted or undone
By those, who, holding, squander or abstain,
Never will one of you rule one of them.
By reason and by nature this is planned,
And you will have the wit to understand . . .

BALTHAZAR. [*Coming up.*]
My father, I wish to speak with you—alone . . .

PRIOR. [*To* THOMAS.]
Leave us.
            [THOMAS *moves away, then hesitates. The*
            PRIOR *looks at him. He disappears.*]

BALTHAZAR. [*To the* PRIOR. *Slowly: with emotion.*]
Yesterday, in the confessional, a man said to me:
"It is five months since old Noll Harding was
killed. They accused his son. He was arrested, tried,
and condemned. But I declare him innocent. It was
I who murdered him." At once, without more re-
flection, but obeying the deepest impulse of my soul,
I bade the man go straight from my presence and
acknowledge his crime . . . He went on to say:
"I had every excuse. My own father's death was
124

caused by old Harding, who poisoned him." I almost drove the man away that he might give himself up as quickly as possible . . . And now, my father, do you understand?

PRIOR.
You have acted rightly.

BALTHAZAR.
And what of me—*me*? Ten years ago I killed my father, *I*, whom you have sheltered here in your midst, without saying a word . . .

PRIOR.
Was this man willing, like yourself, to be
One of our Order, willing on bent knee
To batter with a storm of ceaseless prayer
The doors of Paradise?

BALTHAZAR.   What if he were?
Since yesterday I see by lightning-flashes
Into my soul . . .

PRIOR.   Your crime is blotted out,
Absolved by me, absolved by Rome;
Ten years ago, when you made this your home,
It died in dust and ashes.
Comte d'Argonne, Duc de Rispaire,
At your last hour you will stand up to God,
Indemnified by prayer.

BALTHAZAR.
I would cry out my crime to all the world . . .
By its swift eddies I am caught and hurled
Beyond the reaches of my stubborn will;
I would cry out my crime and earn grace still . . .

THE CLOISTER

PRIOR.
My son . . .

BALTHAZAR.   All night with weary hands I tried
To barricade and break its violent tide;
I could not.   Like a savage sea
It leapt upon me furiously . . .
I had not eyes enough to watch the flood
Of ever-trickling life, and all the blood,
Which drained my father's breast
To deadly stillness.   How the wound gaped wide,
Far wider even now than when he died!
It festered and the fissure grew apace;
With maddened eyes I marked the ceaseless flow
A trickling—trickling—ever-trickling stream.

PRIOR.
A dream!

BALTHAZAR.
Nay, it was blood: real blood reeks so:
I am defiled with it; I know;
I am red with blood, red to the very soul;
It pierces me, it burns me; through my whole
Flesh, like a flame, it runs from heart to head;
I breathe its taint upon me; everywhere
About me wind and air and light are red.
I fear each sudden gleam, each sudden stir;
All things are fearful.   Let the least noise start;
My thoughts, my prayers are paralysed with fright;
And awful silence crushes all the night
Between its iron teeth my bleeding heart.

PRIOR. [*Solemnly.*]
My son, your brain is haunted and distraught.
No longer God, but Satan there

THE CLOISTER

Ruins and rules your thought.
Dom Balthazar, for you he lays the snare
Laid long ago for fervent piety,
For monks, whom rocks and deserts saw surprised
By Pagan devils, yet unexorcised,
For Paul and Anthony.
Your spirit is afire, your soul aflare,
Your haggard feet eschew our paths sublime;
You do not see that theirs is the worst crime,
Who outrage God by doubt and by despair.

BALTHAZAR.
Father!

PRIOR.   Be wise and confident again!
Let soberness and measured calm restrain
Rebellious fury! See that from to-day
Your will is as a scythe to shear away
This evil crop, which bristles with sharp shame.

BALTHAZAR.
Impossible!

PRIOR.   I charge you in God's name.
                    [*In gentler tones, after a pause.*
My son, thou, in our midst, these ten years past,
Hast borne with ecstasy the bloodless fast,
The girdle of pain unseen, the burning smart,
Which, like a sore laid open, stings the heart
To death, to living death, our daily choice,
Our hope of earning Heaven! Christ doth rejoice
Because of thee; His bitter kisses heal
Those wounds sublime, where glorious drops
          congeal;
Lovely to Him is thy self-branding pain,
And angels sing thy penitential zeal.
Now, such a life from God thou durst not steal;

THE CLOISTER

His priest, His harbinger, thou must remain;
Thou canst not by a mad red-raging feat
Cancel the debt of labour incomplete;
Nor thrust, as if thy justice were His law,
Between thyself and Christ a barrier.

BALTHAZAR. [*Agonized.*]
My father! Oh my father!

PRIOR.   Hear my voice!
Leave not the way of pardon—thy first choice—
Which thine advancing feet so simply trod,
That now thy very crime finds favour with God;
He loves it, as the instrument whereby
Thy soul was chosen for especial grace.
If now thy words the heavenly plan confute
And break the ban of silence absolute,
They injure and blaspheme God to His face.
Christ lives indeed for justice, but he died
For pardon: death and pardon are the higher.

BALTHAZAR.
My father!

PRIOR.   Think, too, if this parricide
Be flung as a bone to curs, how each denier
Will suddenly be armed to hurt us all;
And think, no human vengeance may appal
With crimson terror, since thou owest it nought;
And think of me, my son, for I had thought
To make thee chief and master of my power
After my death. Thine is a ruling race;
Thou art elect; thou owest to this place
Thy very life. God knows in what wild hour,
Or why, He brought thee to these walls at last,
Far from thy strange and stormy past,
Humble in spirit, but high and proud of heart.
128

THE CLOISTER

BALTHAZAR.
I have sore need of pity, father!

PRIOR.
Not so: arise! Thy duty is rather
To soar on ample wing; as new crops start,
Spring from the fallow!—Here thou canst repent,
Winning anew the meed of holiness
To heart's content.

BALTHAZAR.
If only now, once and for all, I might
Here, in the chapter-house, my sin confess!

PRIOR.
Old usage gives thee such a right,
To take and make of it an arm secure.
Monks have this licence. But hast thou the might
To repossess thyself?

BALTHAZAR.   Of that be sure!
Before my brethren I shall frankly tear
This red-clawed, evil monster from my brain,
And drown it in their golden-flowing prayer;
I shall go humbly, dazed with joy and pain;
My heart, whose only flowers were grief and fear,
Their honest counsel will wash clean and clear;
I shall entreat them, "Take into your hand
My weary hopes, wan terrors, rage, despair";
I shall hide nothing. Father, you will stand
Beside me?

PRIOR. [*Reassuringly.*]
                   Have no fear, I shall be there . . .
              [BALTHAZAR *kisses the hand of the* PRIOR,
                who goes out. DOM BALTHAZAR *runs
                towards* DOM MARK, *who, for an in-
                stant, had been watching them from far
                off.*

THE CLOISTER

BALTHAZAR.
O Mark, my brother, hearken!—Knowest thou
I shall be born again? night will turn day—
I shall become that man so far away,
Whom thou didst love long since . . .

MARK.   Whom I love now.
For never didst thou forfeit . . .

BALTHAZAR. [*Growing sombre again; sits down and
    turns his face away.*]
                              Hush! my shame
Is still to live and think myself the same.

MARK.
No matter what thy deed, such faith have I
In thy profound, long-noted piety . . .

BALTHAZAR.
Hush! Hush! Say nothing, until I, defiled,
Be pure!

MARK.   My brother, my master, in whose eyes
I am no other than a simple child;
No part of me but flies
Towards thy misery, thy torments wild,
Born of some unknown care:
Here is my heart: lay down thy grief, thy torments
    there!
I am nothing, yet two hands have I
To fold in prayer, two knees to ply
In supplicating saints above;
And with the whole of my wrapt soul
I hail thee, who didst sow my heart with love.
For thee my fervent lips are never still;
I love thee all man may, within God's will;

130

THE CLOISTER

I long to share thine ill, to bear
Thy cross, to feel thine anguish fierce
Fasten on me its violent fangs;
I long for thy transfixing pangs,
Which, like keen lances, thrust and pierce!

BALTHAZAR.
My child!

MARK.   I feel some mystic atmosphere
Around thee; the most perfect of us fall,
Transgressing now and then our rules austere;
But were thy fault most palpable, not all
Hell's heaviest blows could interpose
To stay my love from growing greater still.
Regard me: look into mine eyes,
Full of thy fervour and thy will;
Thou art the magnet, bidding my heart rise
To happy, golden skies;
Thou art the joyful, unassuaged desire,
Which, though it tire, fills life with fire;
Thy witness, after Christ's,
Proves most of all to me that God exists.
Brother, for great deeds marked and manifest,
Rise up, let sorrow be:
Shine, as of old, victorious; in thee
Commandment shows most fair and mightiest.

BALTHAZAR.
Fond soul, spontaneous source
Of kindness, whom I needs must love and bless,
Despite the curbless anguish of remorse,
What naked trust I learned from thee,
What simple goodness, what sweet lunacy!
All nature's simplest tones by thee were taught;
Her accents, on thy fresh lips caught,

131

Mingled with mine, more harsh and passionate;
My haunted soul became less desolate,
Till I believe the message sweet,
Which instinct to thy heart sings secretly;
I think thou guessest God unerringly;
I know thee pure of all malicious heat;
I know thee strict in duty, prompt in prayer,
Chaste as an offering, virginal, and fair . . .

MARK. [*Excitedly.*]
Balthazar! . . . Balthazar!   .

BALTHAZAR.   I shrank alway,
Because thy soul is of such delicate clay,
From fracturing its timid purity;
Else my red secret had been flung to thee;
Thou hadst been told what all will shortly know,—
My shame,—my dreadful sin,—which long ago
Found absolution, but I see it rise
From the black past again;
Again with rampant claws and bloody eyes
It comes to roam and roar through every vein!

MARK. [*Shrinking.*]
I am afraid; say nothing, I implore.
Humble not here thyself to me alone.

BALTHAZAR.
When compline ends, confession shall atone;
And thou wilt hear, wilt say what penance still
May free me from this riotous ill
And put it out of mind for evermore.

MARK.
My soul entire
Shall become fire

132

To watch thy pain above;
And like white linen all my love
Shall swathe thy heart and wipe away each tear;
I hold in hand two weapons shining-clear,
Wild prayer and fervent fast;
These shall contend, till peace be thine at last;
If yet the Holy Virgin, burning now
In fiery trance, be fain to grant my vow;
If she my deepest inmost thought would know,
"Incomparable Mother," I shall cry,
"More bright than rays and roses,
Heal thou my brother's grief and misery!
Be thou to him the raiment that encloses
Both joy and pardon fair,
That one on earth should wear
For God to glance with unshocked majesty
On human woe"!

BALTHAZAR.
My gentle brother!

MARK.   Heaven without thee
Were stripped of gold, of glad eternity;
I wish to save my soul along with thine;
I wish to die, that ardour infinite
May bind us fast in happiness divine;
I wish our destinies might so unite,
That thy lips should with my lips make one sound,
That Jesus and His angels might confound
Thy praise with my praise, when our joint desire
Pours like a torrent in the heavenly fire. . . .
Brother, my brother!
> [*He flings himself on* BALTHAZAR's *breast.*
> *The bell rings.*

BALTHAZAR.   Be no more alarmed.—

THE CLOISTER

Thou hast restored my strength.—Now am I armed
With thy clear spirit against all hell's power.
Already pardon and pity strike their hour,
Already peace rings softly in the bell. . . .
Already confidence complete
Comes to direct along God's path our feet. . . .
Be not alarmed, but pray again. Farewell!

> [*They separate.* BALTHAZAR *goes to* L., *and*
> MARK *to* R.

CURTAIN.

ACT II

The Chapter-house: wooden benches, black and white pavement with a rush mat in the middle. On the wall a crucifix. To the right, in his usual place, kneels DOM BALTHAZAR *with hidden forehead and clasped hands.* THOMAS, *entering, approaches slowly and taps him lightly on the shoulder.*

THOMAS.
YOUR soul is uneasy, my brother. May I not pray and suffer with you?

BALTHAZAR. [*Looks at him and replies with hesitation.*]
All prayers count before God.

THOMAS.
Yours seems no ordinary suffering.

BALTHAZAR.
All the prayers in the world, perhaps, weigh less than my crime.

THOMAS.
Your crime?

BALTHAZAR.
In a moment I shall confess it here before you all.

THOMAS.
Is it so great as to dash your zeal to the ground?

135

THE CLOISTER

BALTHAZAR.
My zeal? What has it to do with my zeal?

THOMAS.
I know the nature of your zeal—tenacious, violent!
I know.

BALTHAZAR.
Leave me . . .

THOMAS.
I know that its secret aim is to dominate these
cloisters!

BALTHAZAR.
Leave me, I tell you . . . Neither you nor I will
be ruler of this House. There are others . . . more
worthy . . .

THOMAS.
Dom Militien?

BALTHAZAR.
Leave me . . . leave me . . . leave me!
              [*Goes to* C. *before crucifix.*

THOMAS.
I no longer understand; I do not know what to
think.
          [*A pause.* BALTHAZAR *makes no reply.*
              THOMAS *continues and goes nearer.*
Dom Balthazar, within our convent wall
You were the chosen man, who came one day
Empowered by God in some mysterious way
To seize by right on our obedience.
Your words were lofty battlements of strength,
Crested with proud pretence;

THE CLOISTER

Your will, by adding stone to stone, at length
In spite of my will overawed us all!
Our Prior heard the call
Of a harsh nature, feudal as his own;
To you should pass at death his place and power.
Life with perplexing, vagrant paths is strown,
But you stood firmly up, a border-tower,
Whence one might see and show mankind
What roads propitious to its journey wind,
And where, through ways of Fate, is drawn God's
    route.
I find you at this hour
Poor, weary, destitute,
A ruin, ruining itself.
Your haughty spirit shakes and falls apart;
Your boldness trembles; what if by-and-by
The vain, colossal pride, which sways your heart,
With sudden crash pay instant penalty?

BALTHAZAR.
If pride this price must pay,
At least 'twas I, who willed and chose the way.

THOMAS.
Ah! There the spirit spoke,
Constrained to utterance by the yoke
Of conscience. Always pride! You and your pride!

BALTHAZAR. [*Distracted.*]
What have I said? It is untrue, untrue!
To love—to love alone—I pay the due
Of agonies, which shall my soul reclaim;
You rob my words and thoughts of every clue;
Your speech, your glances dart
Insidious flame,
Which masters me with treacherous surprise;

But God, who loves and knows me through and
     through,
Into the deep recesses of my heart
Sees clearly with illuminative eyes.
O go your ways, O go your ways!

THOMAS.
You will not have my prayers, then?

BALTHAZAR.   Saints on high,
Whose angel-wings are over Calvary,
Who watched the early Christians wage their wars,
Have pity! See how my repentance soars
Pure of deceit to pardon's mountain-crest.
My brother there in darkness stirs again
With tempter's tongue old pangs of obscure pain,
And sets the old pride bounding in my breast!
But let thy pity, Lord, on him, too, rest,
Pity on him, O Lord, pity on me;
I cannot, will not, even repel one word
Of proffered prayer;
Perhaps, more goodness and more grace are there
Than others pray with—but have pity, pity,
By thy death, by thy baptism, thine agony
Have pity on us, Lord!

THOMAS.
Those prayers for you are mightier that I make
Because, in sueing God for your soul's sake,
I weep and on myself do violence;
More virtue lies
In prayer for those who are our enemies,
Than in red-wallowing gulfs of penitence.
I pray and still shall pray for you.

BALTHAZAR. [*With resignation.*]
I thank you.   [*A pause.*
                    138

THE CLOISTER

THOMAS. [*Moves away and returns.*]
You said to me just now: neither you nor I will be
ruler of this House. And yet, Dom Militien—of high
lineage, I admit—is too old; moreover, he is ill,
shaken, on the verge of death—Idesbald? A mediocrity—Bavon and Theodule? Wretched scriveners,
absorbed in books they do not understand. As for
Dom Mark, a child, an innocent . . .

BALTHAZAR. [*Abruptly.*]
Let be! Let him go free!
He does not know our life
Of violent ambition, infamous strife,
Nor your craft, brother, with his right at odds;
Faith in his own will follows faith in God's;
By angels, not by us, he is chosen chief,
Rising above our mire, a golden sheaf;
When he shall be our ruler designate,
Your lord and mine, to Heaven his heart will cry,
That Heaven itself may reinaugurate
Self-sacrifice, supreme humility.
Since such will be God's will, we shall obey;
Such *is* God's will—providing, if need were,
A miracle for every barrier,
Wherewith you cumber the appointed way.

THOMAS.
Astounding! Let the Prior say point blank:
"To rule and raise the Church, strong men of rank
Are chosen by God, because their force of soul
Condenses to more absolute control,
Being kept and garnered for the common weal,
Persistent, fervent, even when lost to view,
An heirloom, which the centuries seal . . ."
I understand, and think at once of you.
But Dom Mark . . .

139

THE CLOISTER

BALTHAZAR.
Think of him now! Think of him!
> [*Goes towards* L. *to door but turns and listens.*

THOMAS. [*Squaring his shoulders and looking* BAL-
THAZAR *full in the face.*]
I dream of no man's future but mine own.
Your strength in ruin by a fatal whim
Lies spent and prone.
But my strength mounts and utters a great cry;
I am sick of service and humility;
Within my spirit the New Age at length
Triumphs, endowing all her sons with strength
To spurn the time-worn, customary route,
As men reject a dead and sapless fruit.
You others see not how my heart burns clear
With apostolic zeal, God's pioneer!
Monks of proud line and crest armorial,
> [*Pointing to crucifix.*
Christ would decide for me against you all.
Thus would He speak: "You rot in torpid ease
Behind a wall of sleepy pieties;
You vegetate! Far off the trumpets blow
War on my cross, whose wide arms long ago
Embraced the world and pressed it to my heart;
You play an ever-shrinking, sterile part;
Your mantles droop, unlifted by God's air;
You deck my altars, but the beadle there
Can light the candles and dispose the flowers;
You stifle boundless ardours, virgin powers,
The tongues of flame, which on my faithful few
At Pentecost descended. Worthless crew
How often, when I watch you groan and pray,
Drowsing the slow, monotonous hours away,
It seems I should chastise you." . . .

BALTHAZAR. [*Violently.*]   Blasphemy!

THE CLOISTER

Christ said Himself to His disciples, " I
Am in your midst, when ye are joined in prayer."

THOMAS.
His voice and gesture, mind and heart are there,
When those who preach are luminous and wise!

BALTHAZAR.
Monk, we are no less servants in His eyes!
The same fire burns us both with heavenly heat,
But our love seeks Him in some mute retreat
Of holiest peace.   Your dream is to proclaim
Before the blind, deaf world His glorious name,
A world of dust and lust,
Which, like a miser, sick and very old,
Still plays with gold,
And on a painful death-bed will employ
Its utmost will, its utmost skill,
To fabricate some criminal, new toy.
What matters that, compared with truth divine?
With your God and with mine?
"Ah! the apostles and the saints !" you cry ;
Supposing they returned! If suddenly
Out of the grave their stormy spirits came,
Should we not see them fill their hands with flame
To fire the world and reascend the sky?
I know as well as you what doom should be
Wrought on this impious and desolate age,
But never will I bandy words with it,
Infected by its pestilent heritage.
I doubt not that you painfully submit
To contact, which might stain the splendour of
        Christ,
But, pride for pride, mine is less sacrificed.

THOMAS.
Yes, always pride!

141

THE CLOISTER

BALTHAZAR. [*Imperiously.*] Say rather, dignity!
I do not blush to hold my honour high.
I grapple with my crime in vehement strife,
But my soul's stature is thereby no less.
Freed from one crime, myself I repossess,
To crush the evil spirit, that spurs your life;
I pave the way for Mark; I lift him high
On these strong Christian arms to victory.
My burning zeal there is no monk but knows,
And what rude vigour in my bosom glows,
To hinder and repel your mad design.
You make impure the sacramental wine
With dregs of knowledge and with lees of doubt;
So, drop by drop, you pour the poison out,
Which by-and-by will breed destruction.

THOMAS. [*Very coldly.*]   Well,
By pride or penitence, I cannot tell,
Your soul will be its own destroyer, brother.
          [*The* PRIOR *suddenly appears in the Chap-
          ter-house. The two* MONKS *are silent
          and embarrassed. After an instant* DOM
          BALTHAZAR *goes towards him.*

BALTHAZAR.
Forgive the violence, which broke with shame
My spirit's solitude. This mad monk came
To pester me with cares;
And tempt with wicked words my peace of heart.

PRIOR.
Your duty was to drive temptation away,
And muse in austere loneliness apart. [*To* THOMAS.
This man is praying—leave him to his prayers!
          [*The* PRIOR *makes a gesture.* THOMAS
               moves away.

142

THE CLOISTER

We two desire—we only—at this hour
To keep, my son, this cloister's pride and power
Above men's rancour and men's rivalry.
If thy confession be not firm and high,
If it should not restore thee to safe ground
Of general respect and peace profound,
Then it were well to wait and keep silence,
To bridle the stern lips of penitence.
I come to smooth the way, ere thou confess.

BALTHAZAR.
My father, God will easily impress
My strength on others, when amends are made.

PRIOR.
Truly, He is the Lord,—He owes thee aid!
Were I away, if He abandoned thee,
Thy supreme humbleness, and faith rough-shod
Would only injure us and injure God.
Why, if we cannot—two such men as we—
By Christian daring and heroic grace
Keep and defend as ours that holy place,
Which Heaven assigns us by alternate right,
There is an end of merit and of might,
An end of law and order, of the hand
Which rivets on the world its strict command.
Thy rash example is yet kingly-bold.
It must, like holy deeds, shine far and wide,
Till all the brethren, rallied to thy side,
Accept thee, future Master of their fold.
Moreover, I would have these schemers know—
Now—when their plottings to fruition grow—
All that divides them from such men as we,
Who cease not to command—on bended knee!
                    [*The bell rings. Footsteps are heard ap-
                        proaching. The* MONKS *enter the*

THE CLOISTER

Chapter-house.   Each takes his place.
The PRIOR *ascends the pulpit.*

Crucifix.

PRIOR.

		Idesbald.	Militien.		
Monks.	Monks.	Theodule.	Mark.	Monks.	Monks.
		Thomas.	Balthazar.		

PRIOR.
This Monastery has abandoned an old custom, of
which I am reminded by a monk, one of your
brotherhood. Since public confession was abolished,
the moral strength of our order has declined. Ten
years ago, under Dom Gervais, my master and
predecessor, the practice was still in force: I re-
establish it to-day. You are about to hear the
confession of a parricide . . .

THOMAS. [*Rises suddenly and remains standing.*]
A parricide?

PRIOR. [*Continues coldly.*]
Of a parricide, long since forgiven. Before the
world such large and frank avowal would be impossible. But you are monks: you will understand
its beauty and its heroism. You will extol what less
lofty souls than yours could not understand. [*To*
DOM BALTHAZAR.] My brother, make your confession.

BALTHAZAR. [*Rises, and then kneels on the straw
mat in the middle of the chapter-house.*]
First I ask pardon of you all. My crime was committed long ago, and I have lived in these cloisters

144

day after day, year after year, exempt from punish-
ment . . .
My father died: 'Twas I who murdered him.
Coming, one night, home from a dingy tavern,
I felt the wine's wild leaven turn
To madness in my head.
The household slept, but near my father's bed
A solitary light burned red in the dark.
The old man, though enfeebled, yet was stark
And rudely vigorous: I saw his throat
Naked with starting veins: there seemed to float
About his pallid brow a radiance dim ;
Defenceless dignity defended him.
I paused . . .
    Ah! had I for a moment there
Foreseen the life-long anguish of despair
In one flash; had the Christ, whose limbs avouch
      [*Pointing to crucifix on wall.*
Our haggard kisses, kept my father's couch ;
Had one of you—mine own familiar friend—
Been able in those days as now to blend
His heart with mine in prayer's enflaming flood,
Then sin had never stained my soul with blood,
Ne'er had I faced inevitable death . . .

PRIOR.
My son, confess your fault more quietly.

BALTHAZAR.
That instant, big with formidable fate,
My father's eyes were opened; suddenly
He sprang erect to meet my hate;
My throat was all on fire and my breath
Seemed dead. His clutch grew tighter on my arm,
But from his lips no sound betrayed alarm ;
He wished that none should ever know

THE CLOISTER

A name as high as ours had sunk so low.
I felt his brutal fingers grip my flesh
As in a vice; fury flamed up afresh;
Like a fierce animal,
I thrust my father back against the wall . . .
And now the knife glittered before his eyes . . .
So hard his strength was, and so huge his size,
He seemed like all my ancestors in one.
My fingers down his body groped their way
But lost their hold, and always he would shun
The blows I aimed, while his fierce hands at bay
Cut crimson nail-marks deep into my neck.
With all my strength I held him long in check,
Then dashed him to the ground, but he, once more,
Rising with supreme effort from the floor,
Stood, face to face and pride to obstinate pride:
I struck him and he died.
Such, in its bitter, utter loathsomeness,
Such was the foul, mad crime I now confess,
Even as it came to pass ten years ago.

PRIOR. [*Rising.*]
It reeks with blood and shame, yet, even so,
Our convent walls can stifle such a deed.
Here, tuft by tuft consumed, the evil weed
Burns up in golden, penitential fires.
We pass to judgment. Grieve, my son, no more,
But answer, as each questioner requires. [*A silence.*

A MONK. [*To* BALTHAZAR.]
Had your murderous hatred no cause?

BALTHAZAR.
My father was stern and I was wild. He stood like
a barrier between my vices and the wealth they
coveted.

146

ANOTHER MONK.
Did you take pleasure in desiring this murder?

BALTHAZAR.
Ay: long enough to tax my conscience with it.

PRIOR. [*Intervening.*]
The murder was hasty and violent. You cannot
have taken pleasure in desiring, or time in preparing
it. You magnify your fault.

BALTHAZAR.
My shame reaches farther than my sin.

A MONK.
If our reason condemns you, our hearts exalt you.
Your example is magnificently Christian.

IDESBALD. [*Rising.*]
Magnificently Christian? An assassin, then, deserves
an aureole?

MILITIEN. [*Rising too.*]
Dom Balthazar's avowal is sublime!
In olden days, when souls breathed loftier air,
Had such a monk confessed to such a crime,
Besieging God with such perpetual prayer,
Then all his brethren had rejoiced to see
With eyes made holier by his piety
His sin itself to highest Heaven aspire
On flaming wings of penitential fire.

IDESBALD. [*Still standing.*]
Before you saint the sinner, probe his guilt!

MILITIEN.
Ay! draw your sword and plunge it to the hilt!
" Love all men " is no maxim of *your* choice,

THE CLOISTER

If one may judge by that relentless voice.
God from your heart is far away to-night;
Black hatred, like a hard and bitter blight,
So warps you that you hesitate to tell
Your brother he is pardoned. You repel
The guest, who knocks by night at your soul's door.

IDESBALD. [*Pointing to* BALTHAZAR.]
Must *I* be judged? Shall he be judged no more?

THEODULE.
From depth to depth, bewildered and distressed,
My judgment falters.

MILITIEN. [*Turning to* THEODULE.]
                           Crime becomes a test,
A crucial struggle, when transfigured by
Such radiance of God's lightning from the sky,
As struck and woke the apostle in Saint Paul.
Celestial miracles, you forget them all!
Invoking the poor wisdom of a day,
You cast the endless splendour and strength away,
Which filled mad, Christian cloisters anciently.
Christ's home on earth is an anomaly,
Unless we preach this doctrine to the throng:
'Tis heroes set the measure of right and wrong.
Dom Balthazar repents: then, from that time,
Stands higher in proportion to his crime;
The greater his recoil, the more he is strong;—
Not one of us had fought with death so long,
Nor passed victorious each perilous place.
His holy feat sheds light upon his face,
And Heaven shows all of us his sin for a sign,
A mark predestinate of grace divine.
148

IDESBALD.
Mad! You are mad! Was ever wickedness
So boldly praised? He is no more, no less
Than a mere criminal. His looks are wild
And bloody. We renounce him.

A MONK. [*Rises.*]   We are defiled,
As by a leper's touch.

ANOTHER MONK. [*Rises.*]
                         His prayer would mar
Our prayers at the same altar.

ANOTHER MONK. [*Rises.*]   Balthazar
Has strained his eyes on death with look so grim
That they are tainted.

ANOTHER MONK. [*Rises.*]
                         Must we pity him,
When half the shame he cried
Was mixed with pride?

THEODULE. [*Dreamily.*] Nay: casting in His scale
A crime so monstrous, Christ Himself will quail.

PRIOR. [*Rising.*]
Silence! [*All sit down.*] You have ceased to examine a conscience: you wreak malice on the man.
I hoped this confession would be worthy and profit-
able, but it ends in wrangling and hatred. Dom
Balthazar's patience and resignation deserve something more than mere pardon. I invite you to examine, exclusively, his fault; that only, and nothing
else.

THOMAS.
My brother, was your crime known?

149

THE CLOISTER

PRIOR.
We only judge the sin. Crime pertains to human justice.

THOMAS. [*With great calmness.*]
My brother, was your sin known?

BALTHAZAR.
I escaped enquiry. A vagabond was punished in my place. I incurred the shame of seeing him die without saying a word.

PRIOR.
If the judges err, that is their business. Our justice is not their justice.

IDESBALD.
Still we must examine the fault in its full extent.

PRIOR.
Punishment is no part of the fault, but its sequel.

IDESBALD.
Then what penalty remains for him to suffer?

PRIOR.
It is I who decide that.

IDESBALD.
But, in that case, why have you summoned us here?

PRIOR.
To flash on you the light, which heroes cast.
To show you what a soul is like, where Christ,
Lived and enshrined and sacrificed,
Triumphs at last.

150

THE CLOISTER

MARK. [*Ecstatically.*]
Pray without ceasing . . . pray . . . let us pray!

MILITIEN.
Yesterday and to-day Christ is the same.
His power can loose the soul from every snare
And draw it up to Him, like clustering flame.
Our brother was a martyr. . . .

IDESBALD. [*Rising.*]   Nay; a murderer!
I say again, a common murderer!

A MONK. [*Ironically addressing the* PRIOR.]
There are some here, who vaguely would infer
That Balthazar deserves aggrandizement
For his crime's sake. They have the Prior's assent. . . .

PRIOR. [*Suddenly rising.*]
Be silent all! I am sole master here.
Until my body, shrouded on its bier,
Shall lie at rest, where yonder Cross appears,
                    [*He points to the Cross on the wall.*
That guide and ensign of my choice,
You shall hold true each utterance of my voice.
I testify that by heroic tears
And fearless heart
Dom Balthazar has won henceforth his part
In Heaven above of everlasting bliss.
Alone, before you all, what shame was his,
What lowly excess of penitence, though Christ
Required no martyr to be sacrificed!
Yet no one rose and said, with joy at heart,
Knowing he would be understood of all:
"We are but sorry Christians, for our part;
Our souls, complacent and methodical,

151

What are they matched with this soul, mad for
    Heaven?"
I testify as well that rancorous leaven
Chokes up your hearts; suspicious, ill at ease,
Basely you bore yourselves and guiltily;
I hear with ears I still have wit to use
Muttered rebellion, eager to reject
The total trust, the absolute respect,
And blind obedience, which are my dues.
                          [Total silence.
You think, then, by shrewd plots to sap at length
The stone-and-iron basis of my strength?
You think by subtle reasons to impair
The sense of what is written? . . . Speak!
            [He looks round him. Silence. No one
                    moves.
                          I swear,
Here to you all, my hands shall wield their power
Firmly above you, till that ultimate hour,
When my tired footsteps to extinction plod:
Power that shall stand intact, when I am dead.

THOMAS. *[Rising.]*
Know well, in this I hold you warranted.

PRIOR.
I care not. My sole warranty is God.
        [A long pause. The PRIOR *grows gradually*
              calmer and continues.
And now, disperse! *[They rise.]* You have neither
sufficient calmness nor clear-eyed charity to understand and judge your brother.
        [Turning towards DOM BALTHAZAR.
Dom Balthazar, the custom of this monastery demands that I, who presided over this gathering,
where so much magnanimity might have been
shown, should now dictate your penance:

THE CLOISTER

You will sleep on the bare ground, for a month;
You will repeat the Psalms at midnight;
You will keep away from the altar for three days,
and will only hear Mass from the gallery behind the
grating. Obey these commands and peace be with
you!

        [Each MONK *goes out after reverence to the*
Altar.

CURTAIN.

ACT III

The Convent Garden. PRIOR *and* MILITIEN *seated outside door of chapel.*

PRIOR.
I HAVE been thinking of it all night.—Actually, in my presence, the assembly was bitterly divided. Dom Balthazar's confession was an utter failure, our monks . . .

MILITIEN.
Oh, you mastered them splendidly!

PRIOR.
I would sooner have died there and then, in my seat, than abandon Balthazar to them. One and all they flew at him, . . . at *me* . . . And Balthazar did not budge, he refused to defend himself . . . All his strength seemed dead, all his pride crushed.

MILITIEN.
Remorse will eat away the finest energy.

PRIOR.
How fiercely Idesbald opposed us! How soon his evil spirit made way among our monks! How openly they all displayed their audacity, their impatience. It seemed as if this monastery were slipping from my grasp, as if my authority were snapping, like a branch bent and whirled away by the blast.

154

THE CLOISTER

MILITIEN.
You never spoke to them in such tones before.

PRIOR.
And did you notice *their* tone, when they opposed me, did you weigh their answers, their allusions, their defiance? Everything they said implied an understanding, a sudden consciousness of strength. What troubles me most is that they dared not only speak as they did, but think as they did, in our presence, in *my* presence. Some profound change must have taken place in this monastery without my knowing it—even now.

MILITIEN.
When a man becomes as old as we are, his eyes are too dim to see every change.

PRIOR. [*Catching hold of* MILITIEN'S *arm and looking earnestly into his eyes.*]
To think that thirty years ago all was order and submission! When I was elected Prior, you were my only rival, and, when I was nominated, you were the first to obey my orders. Perhaps I should have lacked your wisdom had fortune gone against me. And what good counsel you always gave! . . . Tell me, do you really believe that Balthazar will be my successor?

MILITIEN.
Idesbald is plotting as keenly as Thomas for your place. The day which sees the ruin of Balthazar will separate them and pit one against the other. . . . Until now they have made common cause: it is a good sign.

PRIOR.
Alas! I cannot think you right,

155

THE CLOISTER

Since I begin to doubt my sovereign might;
Authority has lost its brazen clang,
No longer ringing out, as once it rang.
While conscience in their hearts heard silently.
Mine arms grow weak; I am seventy to-night;
I tremble when I lift the monstrance high
Above the crowd. Death tolls within my breast.
I am a tottering wall, a ruined tower,
Whose turrets stand, defiant of death's power;
I shall have been in times of yielding clay
The last great Prior of ancestral sway.
God knows what swirling tide, when I am at rest,
Will sweep this monastery away!   [*A silence.*
I see no other but thyself—no other—Dom Militien,
able to succeed me.

MILITIEN.
I? . . . But if you are vanquished, am not I vanquished too? Am I not weary, ill, useless, on the
brink of the grave? Who can say which of us two
will bury the other? We have done our work in
accordance with God's plan and soon we shall both
depart in peace. [*A silence.*] Besides, when Balthazar
has conquered his own qualms of conscience, he will
triumph over the other.

PRIOR. [*Rises.*]
Oh, I will answer for that. My strength is equal to
that final duty. But what if his own hands should
wreak his ruin? What if he abrogate that magnificent store of energy which he has inherited? There
comes a time when strength, even the surest, in spite
of itself, accomplishes its own downfall. In such a
case, nothing can be done. All is over.

MILITIEN.
You have still Dom Mark.

156

T H E   C L O I S T E R

PRIOR.
He! Never! His hands are only able to pray . . .
                              [*The bell is heard.*
MILITIEN.
Sunday matins are ended.—Here come our monks.

PRIOR.
Go.—It is your turn to sing High Mass. I shall
preach.   [*They disappear.*

The MONKS *enter. Some walk about the arbours, others
        form into groups and converse.*

IDESBALD. [*To* THOMAS.]
Why did you support the Prior so positively? One
should never admit that an opponent is in the right.

THOMAS.
You do not understand.   [*Turns his back on him.*

IDESBALD.
You seem changed since yesterday. I do not recognize you.

THOMAS.
Once more: you do not understand.

IDESBALD.
What? What?—But tell me then . . .

THOMAS. [*Shrugging his shoulders and ignoring* IDES-
    BALD.]
The Prior is right. Authority must remain intact,
supreme. . . . Besides, things move so quickly, that
my attitude is no longer worth discussing. It is
generally approved. Even Theodule approves. He
told me so.

157

THE CLOISTER

IDESBALD.
Theodule?

THOMAS.
The Prior's cynicism opened his eyes.

IDESBALD.
Listen! Supposing I were to inform against Balthazar! A public prosecution would abase him more
utterly than we can, and our monks would bear me
no grudge for it . . .

THOMAS.
A monk can only be judged by monks. If Dom
Balthazar came among us to hide his crimes, the
monastery must give them burial.

IDESBALD.
It would be so easy . . .

THOMAS.
I forbid you to tempt me. . . . Dom Balthazar is
destroying himself. Yesterday I was still thinking of
a way to abase him, but to-day it is useless. Remorse
is a passion for ruin and extinction. We need only
leave him a clear course.

IDESBALD.
You are wrong. Let me do as I say.

THOMAS.
Let you . . . let you do as you say! [*Taking a
sudden decision.*] You shall see. [*Calling the* MONKS
grouped on L.] Brothers, my brothers, listen, all of
you! Someone here advises me to inform the authorities outside the monastery that public punishment

158

THE CLOISTER

may be inflicted for his fault on Balthazar. I wish
you to bear witness that I reject the advice with
horror.

IDESBALD.
Well, but . . .

THOMAS.
I say this before you all: before those who follow
me, and those, if there be any left, who oppose me.

THEODULE.
Your honour was never in doubt.

THOMAS.
I love this monastery. It is my only home. Its
spirit may be old fashioned, but its privileges are
sacred. I shall cherish them as they have never been
cherished before. We are monks, before and above
all.

IDESBALD.
This monastery cannot evade the law.

THOMAS.
You are alone in thinking so. You raise between
yourself and us a barrier more impassable than that
which Dom Balthazar erected. If ever I listened
to your counsels, at this moment I reject them and
separate myself from you.

A MONK.
At last!

ANOTHER.
It was inevitable.

THE CLOISTER

THEODULE.
Idesbald was dangerous: he came between us and you.

THOMAS. [*To* IDESBALD.]
Your plotting was petty, your ambition devoid of greatness. Your spirit wavered uncertainly over books from which I drew strength to strike and wisdom to soar. Our brethren might well fear your influence. When they saw us together, they might think us scheming to betray them.

THEODULE. [*To* THOMAS.]
Henceforth there is nothing to separate us.

IDESBALD. [*Pointing at* THOMAS *and addressing the* MONKS.]
Surely, I must be dreaming. . . . He says this to me, whom he was continually urging . . .

THOMAS. [*To* IDESBALD.]
Let us forget one another. Henceforth, let us pursue different roads.

IDESBALD.
What you say is absurd. It cannot be that in a single day, a single moment . . .

THOMAS.
What must be, will be.

IDESBALD.
Oh! I loathe you even more than Balthazar!

THOMAS.
And I excuse, I pardon you.

160

THE CLOISTER

IDESBALD.

I scorn your pardon. I defy you, face to face, in
this monastery; I will overthrow, one day, the work
of your crafty hands, which now rises to triumph:
I will upset in my turn one day . . .

A MONK. [*Approaching* IDESBALD *and pointing to*
THOMAS.]
All of us here approve our brother Thomas.

IDESBALD.
But you do not know how implacable, how cunning
he is, how his soul . . .

THOMAS. [*To the* MONKS.]
Let him talk: I no longer listen . . .
> [*The* MONKS *withdraw, following* THOMAS
> *and leaving* IDESBALD, *who sinks down
> on a bench, beaten.* DOM BALTHAZAR
> *appearing at the other side of the garden,
> advances and kneels at the foot of the
> crucifix. Scarcely is he at his prayers
> when* IDESBALD *approaches him.*

IDESBALD.
Dom Balthazar!

BALTHAZAR.
What? You?

IDESBALD.
My brother, Balthazar.

BALTHAZAR.
Begone, begone!

IDESBALD.
I come to tell you . . .

M

THE CLOISTER

BALTHAZAR.
I wish to hear nothing . . . I do not wish you to
come near . . .

IDESBALD.
It concerns you; your position in this monastery.

BALTHAZAR.
No: Say nothing, nothing! go away! go away! . . .
> [BALTHAZAR *rises, and drives off* IDESBALD,
> *who at last withdraws.*
>> DOM BALTHAZAR *kneels down once*
>> *more. Scarcely is he at prayer, when*
>> DOM MARK *appears and goes up to him.*

MARK. [*Deeply moved, almost weeping.*]
My brother, it is thy duty to deliver thyself to the
Judge!
> [DOM BALTHAZAR *is astounded. Silence.*
> *Suddenly a light seems to dawn on him.*

MARK. [*Continues.*]
I almost fear to tell thee so,
For my soul, torn with woe,
Aches with each nail thy martyred senses know,
But God claims higher service than love may!

BALTHAZAR. [*Anxiously.*]
Say on! Say on! . . .
> [*His eyes wet with tears, as he gazes on*
> DOM MARK.

MARK.   Would I had known thee on that day,
When public rage and hate
Beheld another lose his life for thee!
O! that I had been he,
That starveling vagabond, whom infamy

162

THE CLOISTER

Banned, but the Cross took safely in,
And a priest shrived his sin;
So had I given life and shed my blood for thee!
I should have died a martyr, silently
Sinking my gentle force in that dim tide,
Which swept thee from man's violence aside;
My peaceful soul on wings of fervent flame
So surely had been borne along
Up to God's angel-throng,
That, praising, I had ever named thy name,
And summoned thee—repentant—reconciled—
To share with me God's golden festival.

BALTHAZAR.
O noblest of our Order, gentle child!
Thy trembling heart, the purest of us all,
Lightens our darkness!

MARK.   Ah! but think of him,
That innocent man, whom Justice, blindly grim,
Despoiled of life and honour! When his heart
In agonizing madness burst apart,
Think how he yearned to reach, to curse
That other,
Whose arm had truly stricken down a brother,
Before God's face, out of the universe;
Think, brother, how his cry must echo shrill,
Demanding thy damnation.

BALTHAZAR.   Oh! be still!
Be still! . . . I have guessed it. . . . I have killed
      two men:
For first I took my father's life and then
I slew that other. . . . In black gulfs of pain
I suffer shipwreck! Verily, my brain
Is dark as a nocturnal vault,

163

THE CLOISTER

Not seeing that Man's justice is concerned
No less than God in punishing my fault.
Oh! I was mad! And always, when I turned
In duty to our Prior for advice,
He fed my folly with glib sophistries,
Lest, otherwise, his Power should come to nought.
Now one thing matters: following one sharp thought
To probe repentance to its uttermost end.
How can I thank thee enough, my child, my friend?
Thy warning led me from false roads aside
And gave my horror-haunted feet for guide
Thy passionate faith, thy white simplicities.

MARK.
With sobs and sighs and litanies
I sued Our Lady, Mother of my Soul,
That, pure and whole,
I might neglect no part of duty's debt!
I love thee! all the more that I must yet
Wound thee and weep to do what yet must be;
I tremble, seeing the massed Calvary
On every cross a monstrous arm extend,
As though it beckoned thee to fearful end!

BALTHAZAR.
Rather rejoice: thou giv'st my soul new life.
My fury, unappeased by futile strife,
Wandered, not knowing on what prey to impress
The cruel teeth of agonized distress.
Now ample fields of penitence display
New vistas to my vision; far away
Salvation now gleams gradually bright.
At last, my feet turn back towards the light!
I am regenerate, since thy radiance came,
Fair as a flower, that trembles into flame,
And shiningly dispersed my dark unrest.

THE CLOISTER

I feel my heart turn golden in my breast.
My conscience is transfigured, so that I
Fear nothing: the sharp blow, the taunting cry,
The bloody axe, are sweet: Death's terror fails,
I will remember how Christ kissed the nails
Upon His gibbet; I will think the word,
Absolving my mad grief, by thee is heard,
And, when my strangled body at last shall fall
Prone on the scaffold, God will hear thy call.

MARK.
Alas, my brother!

BALTHAZAR.   Though I suffer, still
Death will be red and Christian! If God will,
No shock shall lay that rocky courage low,
Whereon His name is carven; I will show
With what calm brow, what vast tranquillity
Even to-day a priest still dares to die!
At last I feel, while all those tempests cease,
The dawning grandeur of a soul at peace.
Why does death wait? Already I can hear
Confessors whisper pardon in mine ear;
I hear already martyred saints, who wait
High up to comfort me, at Heaven's gate.
"Open!" I cried to them: "Lo, I am he,
Who from the land of darkness comes back home,
That land, where crimes, like flaming lions, roam;
Lo, I am he, who now comes back
From the remotest track
Of his soul's panic misery,
Saved by a child, whose gentle art
Through love and prayer so brightly fired his heart,
That by the old baptismal way
Towards the angelic hosts he mounts to-day,
Where heroes, saints and martyrs dwell apart!

165

THE CLOISTER

I am he, who vanquished and put hatred by,
Yet, being enchained by human sophistry
And holding right to be *his* right, demurred
To pay the total price, by crime incurred.
O wondrous Heaven, infinitely deep,
Where crimes are burned asleep,
Into your flames, by pity and pardon fanned,
I fling myself to the furnace as a brand;
I reach your golden threshold, knowing not
If vanquished or victorious my lot,
Unheralded and unescorted quite,
Save that my grief and this child's grief unite. . . .
                              [*He points to* DOM MARK.
Enough! the air of this earth stifles me;
The wind is drunk with blood and blasphemy;
I long for instant death, for instant life.

MARK.
And I, my brother?

BALTHAZAR.   O gentlest of friends!

MARK.
First must thou suffer penance, make amends. . . .

BALTHAZAR.
No! No! Christ must not wait: his flames are lit.
I will not for a dismal rule remit
That hour, which shall behold me saved and free.
Brother, farewell, farewell! Only in thee
I have found a soul, where highest truth has part.
Soon all my fault in all my blood will drown.
From Heaven, with outstretched soul, I shall look
    down.
Farewell!   [*He hastens away.*

THE CLOISTER

MARK. [*Falling on his knees and hiding his face in his hands.*]
I entrust thee, brother, to God's heart!
> [*The bells ring. The* MONKS *enter the church.* DOM BALTHAZAR *returns, hesitates, and suddenly takes a decision. The worshippers enter by the garden-gate to hear Sunday Mass. He mixes with the stream, as they pour into the porch.*

CURTAIN

ACT IV

*The Chapel. On the right the altar. Facing the
audience, the barred recess in which* DOM BAL-
THAZAR *does penance. Under this recess a door.
To the left the pulpit. Near the door, on the wall,
an enormous Crucifix.*

> DOM MILITIEN *at the altar is finishing Mass.
As he intones "*Ite Missa est*" and turns away
towards the sacristy, the* MONKS *reply:* "Alleluia."
> *The* PRIOR *slowly ascends the pulpit.*
> *The* MONKS *are massed near the altar-rail in
three rows. The* WORSHIPPERS *are grouped behind
them, reaching across the stage to the pulpit.*

PRIOR. [*Making the sign of the Cross.*]
IN the name of the Father . . . and of the Son . . .
> [*As the worshippers are on the point of leaving,
a great noise is heard in the recess, where*
DOM BALTHAZAR's *haggard face is seen
behind the bars.*

BALTHAZAR. [*In the barred recess.*]
I killed my father! I killed my father!
And here am I, shut in,
Like a wild beast within a cage,
To stifle the mad din
Of my fierce soul's remorse and rage!

PRIOR.
Unhappy man!
> [DOM MARK *throws himself at the foot of
the Crucifix, and remains there in
supplication throughout the scene.*

168

T H E C L O I S T E R

BALTHAZAR. [*To the crowd.*]
I am the Friar Balthazar!
My crime is a tempestuous flame,
Which bites and burns my soul with righteous
    shame;
I am that Friar Balthazar,
Who, your confessions being said,
Fiercely on faults and vices fell,
And all the while with secret guile
Beneath his hair-shirt kept and fed
His own damnation, his own hell.

PRIOR.
This is a madman! Pay no heed!

BALTHAZAR.
My father, kind in word and deed,
Bore gently with each furious excess;
One night I killed him, as you kill a dog,
With drunken callousness.

PRIOR.
Pay him no heed! Pay no heed!
As God is living, pay no heed!

BALTHAZAR.
A guiltless man, to death condemned,
Upon the scaffold took my place;
He prayed to God, he cried for grace,
He kissed in vain the Cross of Christ;
I coldly saw him sacrificed,
And, without moving, watched him die.
A glance, a word, a single cry,
The flaming of the sword had stemmed,
But that one word, which found no breath,
Between my teeth was crunched to death.

THE CLOISTER

PRIOR. [*Indicating* BALTHAZAR *to the* MONKS.]
Tear him down by force from the tribune!
[*The* MONKS *move towards the tribune.*

BALTHAZAR.
I am the Friar Balthazar!
Lord of Argonne and of Rispaire:
Oh! these are murderous hands of bloody hate,
More ravenous than any maw;
Behold them: see, what hands are there!
The sovereigns of the law
In their tribunal did not dare
To scent the blood indelible,
Which, obstinately washen, steeped my hand;
But you, to-day, all you who understand,
Go forth among the townsfolk, forth and tell,
Proclaim it well . . .

PRIOR.
Such repentance is a scandal.
[*Blows of a hatchet on woodwork are heard.*

BALTHAZAR.
My soul is as a thicket of black sin,
Where every sacrilegious thorn
Curves back on me and drives black talons in;
The holy mantle I have worn
Becomes a lie: it serves to hide
The leprous, fetid flesh inside;
Evil in me is like a lustful flame,
The lips of men no more should speak my name;
I bid the whole world curse me and deride;
I bid you all spit in my face;
Cut off these hands, which wrought such murderous
    spite;
Tear off this mantle's prostituted white;

170

THE CLOISTER

Call out the mob, stir up the populace!
On me let their worst fury dash:
I give myself for fists to crash,
My brow for stones to gash;
I bid them crush and batter in
This body, burdened with implacable sin;
I bid them throw, when torturing fires shall flag,
To the four winds this human rag!

> [*The* MONKS *succeed in breaking the door
> and seizing* BALTHAZAR. *Great uproar.
> At once the* PRIOR *addresses the crowd.*

PRIOR.
Go out, all of you!

> [*The* MONKS *thrust the crowd to the door
> of the Chapel.*

Go out, all of you! Balthazar is reserved for the
thunderbolts of God.

> [*The nave empties slowly. The* MONKS *who
> had gone up to the tribune, bring* BAL-
> THAZAR *down and fling him on his
> knees before the* PRIOR *in the middle of
> the church. The* PRIOR *approaches him.*

PRIOR.
Thou friar Balthazar,
Thou hast made mockery of Christ,
Who wills that man should silently repent;
Our holy rules, our cloister's high intent
By thee are violently sacrificed;
Out of thy brain all meekness fades away;
Thou art as deaf and blind as iron is,
Not seeing with that drunken soul to-day
Thou rollest downward into Hell's abyss.

BALTHAZAR.
My God! My God!

171

THE CLOISTER

PRIOR.
The blood, that stained thy father's face,
Stains all our walls to-day with crimson flake,
Thy wild-beast cunning sought a hiding-place
Here, to pollute our cloister for thy sake!

BALTHAZAR.
My God! My God! My God!

PRIOR.   Hear what I say!
I had intended thee, when once my soul
Stood before Christ above, on life's highway
To follow in my steps, to play my rôle
Through strife and prayer and grim emergency.
God has restored my sight. I have my lesson.
He has shattered like a wreck on a wild sea
Before mine eyes the white, proud galleon,
Loaded with bales of myrrh and incense pure,
Which thou appearedst; windy fury now
Has stripped of holy oil's investiture
Thy brow, no more a gilded priestly brow.
To me thou seemest damned more utterly
Than if thy body in fire were sepulchred;
Thy crime's ungovernable memory
Shall never cease to make its clamour heard;
No prayer shall ever to thy frantic call
Respond with flaming tongue;
And, being dead, for thy soul last of all
Shall holy Mass be sung;
Ay, and this crozier, . . . [*He raises it threateningly.*
                          Which thy dream did crave
To wield with virile mastery, There! there!
                          [*He strikes at him.*
Thy flesh shall feel how hard it is to bear,
Not as a sceptre, but a common stave.

172

THE CLOISTER

BALTHAZAR.
Strike! Strike! Strike! my father!

PRIOR. [*Flinching, supported by the* MONKS.] Ungodly! Ungodly! Ungodly!
> [*Without perceiving it, he lets the crozier
> fall from his hands.*

A MONK. [*Approaching.*]
Murderer of Christ!

ANOTHER MONK.
Thief of repentance!

ANOTHER MONK.
Ruffian!

ANOTHER MONK.
Parricide!

THEODULE.
Blasphemer!
> [THEODULE *thrusts* BALTHAZAR *aside with
> his foot, causing him to fall back with
> his face to the ground.*

PRIOR. [*Bracing himself up for a last effort.*]
No: lift him up: thrust him beyond the gate,
Beyond the walls, immediately,
Towards shame and horror and the last abyss!
> [*The* MONKS *lift* DOM BALTHAZAR *and
> drive him before them as far as the
> church door, which they shut behind
> him noisily.*
And now for evermore be separate
173

THE CLOISTER

His lot from ours, and may his mad crime's weight
Fall with more crushing horror on his life
Than even the scaffold's knife.

> [*A long silence. At last* THOMAS *having
> picked up the crozier, advances towards
> the* PRIOR. *At this moment all the*
> MONKS, *except* IDESBALD *and* DOM
> MARK, *form a group round* THOMAS.

THOMAS. [*Looks intently at the* PRIOR.]
My father!

PRIOR. [*After a silence.*]
Be it so!

> [*Pointing to the door by which* BALTHAZAR
> *has gone out.*

Since he refused his right, since he denied
The power in himself personified;
Since now among you all I find at length
Not one of my stature, not one of my strength;

> [*Pointing at* THOMAS.

Do you at least defend, with Heaven's accord,
These cloisters in the ruthless days to be!

> [THOMAS *gives back the crozier to the* PRIOR
> (*all this seems to take place mechanically*).

MARK. [*Left alone in front of the crucifix.*]
Out of the depths of thy great mercy, Lord,
Show helpful charity
To Balthazar, the brother of my soul;
Thou only knowest the whole,
And what new'lot in Heaven remains,
Won by his penitential pains;
Lord, aid him at this moment, when
His foes are furies, masked as men;

174

THE CLOISTER

The world, a cruel, mud-bespattering horde;
His brethren, a calumnious frown;
To soothe his crimson agony, O Lord,
Send angels down!

CURTAIN.

PHILIP II

A TRAGEDY IN THREE ACTS

TRANSLATED BY

F. S. FLINT

NOTE

PHILIPPE II, first published in 1901 (Paris, "Mercure de France"), was produced at the Théâtre du Parc, Brussels, in the same year and at the Théâtre de l'Œuvre (Nouveau Théâtre), Paris, in May, 1904.

Like an Elizabethan play of our own theatre, it is written in prose and verse; but the verse, which, following the French tradition, is rhymed, has occasional irregular periods, known loosely as *vers libre*. In this translation, while endeavouring to give an exact rendering of the original, I have sought to produce a play as near the English tradition in form as possible, preserving, however, in faithfulness to the original, the periods of *vers libre*.

F. S. F.

DRAMATIS PERSONAE

PHILIP II, *King of Spain.*
DON CARLOS, *Infante, Prince of the Asturias.*
COUNTESS DE CLERMONT, *maid of honour of the court.*
FRAY BERNARDO, *confessor of the King.*
DON JUAN OF AUSTRIA.
DON FRANCISCO DE HOYOS, *notary of the King.*
FRAY HIERONIMO.
COUNT DE FERIA.
SOLDIERS AND MONKS.

The action for all three acts takes place at the Escurial.

PHILIP II

ACT I

A terrace. On the left, the pavilion of DON CARLOS.
*In the background, the Escurial, in which one
window only, that of* PHILIP II's *apartment, is lit
up. Between the background and the terrace the
gardens of the palace. Two stairways, one right,
the other left, descend from the terrace to the gardens.*

DON CARLOS.

G OD! how my body is dull and sick this evening;
How mournful yonder on the countryside
Is the light of the nights of Spain.
Rigid and black, the Escurial
Throws a more dismal and a darker shadow
Among the many other shadows
I watch, and that see me die. . . .
Oh! my locked dream I fear even to half-open.
Oh! my desires: steeds prancing in the gold of
    glories. . . .
            [*He walks to the edge of the terrace and
                            waits.*
Yesterday, I was steadfast and serene,
My being quivered like a sword
New-planted in its victory;
I was half mad; my footsteps entered
The immense future with so great an ardour
That my grandsire himself had loved their fury.

183

PHILIP II

And now as ever I am gloomy and sad,
Incredulous of my triumph. . . .
> [*Turning in the direction whence the* COUN-
> TESS *will come.*

Alas! why does she not come? [*Suddenly, violent.*
Why does she not come then, since I will it so!

THE COUNTESS. [*Appearing at the left stairway.*]
Carlos! my king Carlos?

DON CARLOS. [*Throwing himself into her arms.*]
                    O my beloved!
O sweetness of thy voice! O beauty of thine eyes!

THE COUNTESS. [*Rapidly.*]
The Marchioness d'Amboise is saved. At this
moment she is crossing the sea. The English
Protestants await her. Thy orders have been carried
out. Oh! that is a kind deed thou hast done, my
king!

DON CARLOS. [*Absently.*]
Ah!   .

THE COUNTESS.
Thou dost not regret it?

DON CARLOS.
Oh! how my heart is tired and sick this evening!
My pallid body is the drinking-place
That aches and fevers dry.
Sly evil grips me, over my lips death hovers.
My old wound burns me still.
Belovèd! Oh the brightness of our love
And the life-giving drops sealed in thy kisses!

PHILIP II

THE COUNTESS.
Carlos!

DON CARLOS.

        Oh! why art thou not always near me,
With thy starred soul and beauty,
With thy tranquillity, with thy large faith,
To stay my spirit that falls, but ever rises,—
Starts up again and gluts itself with pride.
I am Carlos of Spain : I bear
The grief, the ache, and the sad splendour
Of an impatient dream which I have cherished
For years, and which remains
Captive within my heart that bounds
Towards rapid glory and triumphs nigh at hand.
I have no time for lingering; the bells
That will ring out my death
Must first of all
Cry my release and greatness to the world.
Oh! Charles the Fifth, I am a stone in thy sling.
I am a glowing weapon that must serve!

THE COUNTESS.
At last, thou dost remember, Carlos!

DON CARLOS.
A while ago I fled from thy words. I was lifeless.
I no longer dared to think of the boldness of my
plans. And yet, from to-morrow, they become
reality. Everything is fixed, promised, arranged.
Don Juan's help alone is still lacking. [*A pause.*]
He promised thee to help us save the Marchioness
d'Amboise. Has he done so?

THE COUNTESS.
When the marchioness reached Guipuzcoa, she
made for Renteria and Passagès. Don Juan, general

185

of the sea, thanks to a chance order received from the King himself, sent away his ships. The coast was free. A bark was brought in, and the marchioness was able to fly from Spain. Thus, without seeming to favour us, Don Juan helped us.

DON CARLOS.
Good.

THE COUNTESS.
You know how I love the marchioness, and how I trembled at the knowledge that she was in Madrid. King Philip surrounded her with snares; he suspected her of heresy.

DON CARLOS.
It was not my father, but the monks, that were to be feared; they alone are to be dreaded.

THE COUNTESS.
Alas!

DON CARLOS. [*Abruptly.*]
Not so, not so! They are the divine foundation that upholds my power; they are the blood, the heart, the strength of Spain. If ever remorse assails me for having saved the marchioness, they it is who will awaken it. . . . Truly, I must love you more than myself; I must love you blindly; I must love you like a sin. . . .

THE COUNTESS. [*Tenderly.*]
Forgive me.

DON CARLOS.
Come nearer to my heart and to my lips that I may
    forget.

PHILIP II

The Holy Inquisition is salvation, dear one.
Into its mashing-vats of fire the world's lees
Are poured and lost and burnt in the face of God,
Who makes the flame to save the universe.
The Church's wild magnificence must not cause
Thee fear; it has transformed itself into
A lioness that with terror, love and anguish
Buries its burning teeth in impious flesh.
Its right is sovereign, though its strength be bloody.
Rome is of use to all, especially kings;
All fear and follow her—and I alone
Bear in my heart enough of fertile ardour
To be at the same time both Spain and Church
And the world also in myself alone.

THE COUNTESS.
Thou art overwrought, Carlos.

DON CARLOS. [*Furiously.*]   No, no, no! . . .
My head is beating with such marvellous floods
Of pride that there is nothing that I fear.
The power of kings will take date from my reign.
This palace near completion, like a mountain,
Is too big for my father; it fits me.
I will have painted on its walls the fury
Of my fought battles and my golden ships
Piercing the oceans and the wild horizons
With the leaps forward of their conquests;
An immense bruit of fame will greet my footsteps.
The sea and sun are mine; the earth is ready;
And I shall not die, since I will not so. . . .

THE COUNTESS. [*Almost pityingly.*]
Carlos! Carlos!

PHILIP II

DON CARLOS. [*Becoming calm.*]
Ask Don Juan what dreams we built up together,
and how much faith our hearts had in our destinies.
We promised each other fame, and we shall both
acquire it.

THE COUNTESS.
Will he come?

DON CARLOS. [*Nods assent and continues.*]
With what gladness will he follow my fortunes. He
has long suspected my desires; but he does not
know yet what I wish to attempt, without further
hesitation, to-morrow. [*Suddenly unnerved.*] I can
no more . . . I can no more . . . I must fly this
moment from here to Flanders.

THE COUNTESS. [*Dragging him to the edge of the
    terrace. The lamp in the* KING'S *window goes out.*]
Look there how great and lovely is night in the
    distance
And how divine is silence on the earth!

DON CARLOS. [*Allowing himself to be persuaded.*]
O soothing, pure and serene light!
O splendour of the pallid mountains, yonder! . . .
The Escurial is sleeping and its gardens
Are weary of too great beauty in midday's flame.
Madrid is white; the steeples of Our Lady
Among the box and cypress trees mount up,
Far off, and slowly the ancient Manzanarès
Tells to its reeds the legends of old Spain.

THE COUNTESS.
A silver softness falls upon the fields!
O my beloved, how good it is to live,
188

PHILIP II

And how my arms desire to be for ever
The sanctuary for thy weary forehead
And for thy stormy heart. I came to thee,
Maternal, docile, from my plains of France
Where love is without terrors, where the sky
Smiles on life kindly, where the hours
Spent on the clemency of love are followed
By no unhealthy dream, nor any fears.

DON CARLOS. [*Trustfully.*]
How lovely are thine eyes! how great thy soul!

THE COUNTESS.
Thy glory and thy triumph have that soul
For flame. I dream of thee, like the white Valois,
Installed in bright and joyous palaces,
Yonder amid a verdant leafage, free
To act as master and to will as king.

DON CARLOS.
I love far skies and hardy enterprises. . . .

THE COUNTESS.
The air of the Escurial is pestiferous
With muffled violence and with dull constraint.
We do not live there, Carlos, we await death.
When night falls around us, the winds ring out
I know not what call towards a train of sorrow
In black and gold that from here covers Spain.
Deserts of burning sand, harsh mountains, valleys,
A dry, unruffled cruelty enwraps them;
Everywhere uniform, it seems to be
A parcel of their nature; and the soil
Is at the same time frost and burning heat,
And nothing grows in it but evil desires. . . .

PHILIP II

DON CARLOS.
How often have I felt the loathing of it,
The anguish, in those hours of rage and fever,
When madness lit my nights with all its fires.

> [*At this moment* PHILIP II *appears at left
> stairway, advances very slowly towards*
> DON CARLOS *and the* COUNTESS, *and
> stands behind them without their seeing
> him.*

But now I have thy fervour and thy soul
And the lake of our love to drown my cares in.
Thy words are radiant to me, and the flames
Of thine eyes are as sweet to me as blessings.
Hearken now. There is silence about our joy;
Thy room is peaceful, and thy body is
My prey. Belovèd, hearken, come away . . .
Come. . . . Come. . . .

> [DON CARLOS *drags the* COUNTESS *away.
> They both go towards the room.*

THE COUNTESS. [*Turning.*]
The King!

> [PHILIP II *looks at them, makes a vaguely
> reassuring gesture, and continues his
> nocturnal walk; he disappears by the
> right stairway without speaking.*

My blood flowed back
Into the deepest of my being.

DON CARLOS. [*Going to the balustrade to see.*]
                                        Yet
His lamp was out; he seemed to be asleep. . . .

> [*Suddenly violent.*

O false nocturnal king who spied on us,
Violent, gloomy king, whose every step
Crushes, it seems, a portion of my heart;

190

PHILIP II

O king of anger and silence, king of horror,
King my father, whose scarlet sins are numbered
By all the cries, despairs, and all the terrors,
That howl their folly in the winds of the world,
I call on God to witness that I, thy son,
Have every right to flee thy unclean clasp,
And twist the arm that seeks to stifle me.

THE COUNTESS.
Carlos! Carlos!

DON CARLOS. [*Panting.*]
               I want the whole of life;
I want to suffer, and to die
That I may triumph.
If I am weary, it is because my strength
Is fettered fast; it is because the Escurial
Holds me; it is because the king has cast
His mortal shadow over all my ways.
What soul could have withstood this constant
    torment?
My very house, unwitting, was accomplice:
Equerries, major-domo, pages, servants;
But now I rise again upon the heights
Of my own pride and destiny;
I have to aid me always both
My stubborn hate
And thy firm love,
And I am drunken
With all the hope
That thy most marvellous and secret power
Fosters within my being.
        [DON CARLOS *has gradually approached the*
          balustrade of the terrace. Suddenly, he
          starts, and, clutching the COUNTESS,
          points to the courtyard of the Escurial.

PHILIP II

Come here, look there!
    Thou seest that black monk who seems as though
by chance to have reached the corner where the
king disappeared? Well, that monk is the spy of
the Holy Inquisition. Philip II watches; but he is
watched over. Each step he makes towards us,
someone makes towards him. Look, he is going in
and the monk disappears.   [*To himself.*
O ever watchful, ever sovereign power!

THE COUNTESS.
The king is everywhere invisible
And hostile: he is in these corridors,
These towers, these gardens; he can see between
The joints of walls; his sudden eyes, that take
Our bodies for their butt, our souls for target,
Make hidden watch upon us day and night.
They look on life as if it were sin itself.
Oh! Carlos, if we were not sure of ourselves,
If a supreme fervour did not burn in us,
They would freeze up our hearts and reign in us.

DON CARLOS.
Be without fear. I have my bold, immense
Designs, shining with hope and glory and anger.
I shall be king to-morrow. I know what must
Be done to get to Flanders and from there
To gain to my side, since my cause is theirs,
Both France and the Empire. Ah! my father, never
Wilt thou find curses sharp enough to curse
The day whereon I was inflamed by thee.

THE COUNTESS.
Here comes Don Juan. Good-bye . . . my heart
    shrinks,
My heart that ever on thy lips will hover. . . .
           [*She goes out.*

PHILIP II

DON CARLOS. [*To himself.*]
The King has faith in him and listens to him.
He does not know Don Juan's love for me.
My father. . . .

> [*He turns, sees* DON JUAN *before him, who*
> *salutes him.* DON CARLOS *imperiously.*

I wish to fly from Spain. I want
Your help, unhesitatingly, to-morrow.

> [*Calming himself.*

Don Juan, thou rememberest
Our youthful passions, our twin ardours,
The dreams we gladly shared
When in Alcala years ago
We lived together
And side by side;
Our hearts were hearts of equal boldness
That Charles the Fifth held in his lofty hand.
Thou didst divine then what prince I would be,
And in what dreadful fate my life would seethe.
Thou didst not love my father, and I loathed
    him.
Oh! our hatreds, oh! our unappeased rages.
Afterwards thou didst leave me, at my advice,
To take thy place where none can do thee hurt,
And reign, both in the tempest and the sunshine,
Over the sails and cannons of my ships.
Thou wert the master of the seas, while I,
With sulking heart and brain that can but dream,
With feet bound to the weight I bear, I still
Am, like a child, a subject of the king.
He rings me round with honours and with spies;
He thinks I do not apprehend the insult
Of his favours, that I will always suffer
His pompous contumely. By shifty ways
He acts, and I by leaps. Canst understand
My fury and my tense desire to bite?

PHILIP II

DON JUAN.
Carlos!

DON CARLOS.
      My confidence in thee is still
As great as when, in the mad years gone by,
That nearly saw my reason founder, thou
Didst call me brother, and I loved the name
Among the many words of thy affection.
Thou wert more to me than a prince, and more
Than a companion; thou wert mild and helpful,
And before thee, one day, I dared to weep,
In my distress, freely and without fear.
Those times of evil and misfortune now
Are far away, but may return again
If my relentless father will it so.
Cunning and torture in his brain take flesh.
At night he passes in my dreams; I feel him
Walking towards my repose by a bloody path,
To caress my brow, my eyes, my neck, my throat,
With his long hands that strangle suddenly,
And with his treacherous fingers, with his fingers
Of fear and darkness . . . Ah! since I am I
Canst understand that I cry out and bite!

DON JUAN. [*Spontaneously.*]
Ah! indeed!

DON CARLOS.
Philip II was still Infante, like me, when he first
governed Flanders. He forced his father to make
way for him. I follow his example. For a long time
I have remained silent, but I have now arrived at
the age of command, and, when you are a prince of
Spain, of rule.
    Let the King nominate the Duke of Alva, what
matter! I appoint myself.

PHILIP II

DON JUAN.
That is rebellion, Carlos.

DON CARLOS.
Berghes and Montigny foresaw my development
and saw clearly. They counselled me to take by
force what was refused as my right.

DON JUAN.
Berghes and Montigny are dead.

DON CARLOS.
Berghes died in time. Montigny was killed. I keep
their memories. But there remain all the lords of
Flanders. Brederode, Horn, Egmont, uphold my
quarrel. I have only to make my appearance to find
an army. They have promised, and the army is
ready; it only awaits its chief, myself.
   If I hesitate, Antwerp, Brussels, and Ghent are
lost to Spain. The Duke of Alva is detested there.
His presence would be the signal for revolt and our
shame. The name of William of Orange grows in
power, and the people seize upon it. They are
forgetting that of Charles V. Neither the Queen
Regent nor Granville resists; they are at the end of
their resources.

DON JUAN.
How well-informed thou art!

DON CARLOS.
I have reflected on my victory more than thou
thinkest. Like thee, when thou didst hurry to fight
the Turks, I am intoxicated with strife and battles.
Thou art as devoted to me as any. Only yesterday
thou didst save with me the Marchioness d'Amboise.
When do we start together?

PHILIP II

Don Juan.
But I cannot . . . I do not wish to . . . I . . .

Don Carlos.
I need thy ships and thy men. I will make for
France, and then Flanders. The Valois support
my cause. They detest Philip. Ghent, Brussels,
Antwerp will be my towns, as they were Charles
the Fifth's.
Oh! Don Juan, dost thou hear the frantic bells
And belfreys, and the shouts and the triumphant
Receptions in the heart of lovely Flanders?
I will make it love Spain by appeasing it.
Philip the Second kills it to subdue it;
I will equal him in firmness, but our right
Will bear a prouder lightning in its hands;
My language will at least be frank and honest:
I shall not lie; and I shall give as pledge
For my vows, my revolt against the King!

Don Juan.
Thou art Infante of Spain; thou canst not in face
of the world and of thy father. . . .

Don Carlos.
Louis XI, French Dauphin, did as I am doing.

Don Juan.
But thy dream is a crime. If thou dost not succeed,
thou destroyest thyself for ever.

Don Carlos.
Charles V always succeeded.

Don Juan.
Never would he have thrown his rights to chance.

196

PHILIP II

DON CARLOS.
He would have understood me . . . still, let be;
I will hear nought; the Duke of Alva never
Shall get to Flanders. Now it is too late
To stop me or perplex me. Thou wilt lose
Me or wilt follow me, I swear it: choose,
Choose!

DON JUAN. [*Hesitating and seeking his words.*]
        Oh! Don Carlos, if I could, if I . . .

DON CARLOS.
Thou dost detest as much as I this duke,
This evil duke . . .

DON JUAN.   Wait. If I could . . . so sudden,
So terrible a venture, so . . .

DON CARLOS.   What? What?

DON JUAN. [*To himself.*]
Perhaps . . . and all would thus come right . . . the
    King . . .

DON CARLOS.
What dost thou mean? Say . . . say. . . . What
    stratagem . . .

DON JUAN. [*To himself.*]
The King . . . must know . . .; surely . . . he
    will understand . . .

DON CARLOS. [*Impatiently.*]
So, I shall go to Flanders with thy help?

PHILIP II

DON JUAN. [*With decision.*]
Still better! I hope one day to lead thee there
Myself. Brave schemes have never found me
    trembling;
The more they appear daring, the more glorious.
My boldness is alert, my courage ready:
I will act quickly. Meanwhile, trust in me.
                              [*He goes out.*

DON CARLOS. [*To the* COUNTESS, *who enters.*]
Victory, sweetheart! We possess its lightning!
Don Juan is mine. Don Juan consents to all.
To-morrow, the whole sea acclaims the flight
Of our sails towards my northern territories.
I will set up thy splendour and thy grace
On board an eager galleon finely built;
Our love will proudly shine there; and our right,
Floating far-off upon the treacherous waves
Will with the golden flashes of its youth
Dazzle, even in this dull and monstrous palace,
The King!

THE COUNTESS.
              Belovèd, I am wild with joy
To feel thee free and rescued by our love.
Don Juan then has fixed for thee the day
And the bright hour . . .

DON CARLOS.   Don Juan gave his word.
We shall make Antwerp; and he too would share
The joyous dangers that will fill my life.
His mind is clever and his heart unswerving . . .
What we must do, he will inform us later.
198

PHILIP II

THE COUNTESS. [*Anxiously.*]
Meanwhile, what will he do? What are his plans?
Will he act suddenly so that thy father
Knows nothing till thou hast arrived in Flanders?

DON CARLOS.
Don Juan told me nothing: thy surprise
Will be to see, not understanding it,
The plan succeed.

THE COUNTESS.   Not understanding it,
I fear.

DON CARLOS. [*Astonished.*]
        Hast thou no confidence? Alas!
How quick this strange doubt would perplex in me
The courage that I need to take me through.

THE COUNTESS. [*Recovering herself.*]
No, no, my heart speaks not in what I said;
My hope is whole, and nothing alters it.

DON CARLOS. [*Downcast.*]
Alas! I saw it all as if accomplished,
And on the golden roads that sway the earth
Our feet unfettered take their wondrous flight . . .

THE COUNTESS.
That which thou seest alone exists.

DON CARLOS.   Not so! Not so!
Oh! how my body is heavy and full of woe!
Everything shuns my looks and flies from me;
Darkness and night alone I feel about me;

PHILIP II

One moment takes back what another gives.
Alas! thy love even wavers and forsakes me;
I flinch and fear, and suddenly I see,
As in a black and hungry pit, my rights
Founder.

THE COUNTESS. [*Ardently.*]
        What thou seest is thy youth, thy courage,
Thy glory and the universe
Saved by thee from the lightnings
Of the dread and mortal storm
Let loose by Philip
That he would swell.
Thy pride it is to seize once more,
By deeds of fertile hate and daring,
From the dead hands
But tragic still of Charles the Fifth
The golden sceptre that made Spain the world!

DON CARLOS. [*Recovering himself.*]
O the great memories that throng my brow!
O words that burn in me like flames! O all
That sings within my heart in unison
With thy soul's wondrous and reverberate voices.
I breathe in courage as I lean towards thee;
And all my hopes are re-born in thy presence.
How lovely is the night and tense the silence!
How beautiful thine eyes are when they love
Their king!

THE COUNTESS.
        Come, let us love each other, Carlos.
Night is the ornament of fire and darkness
Surrounding love. The ancient Manzanarès
Murmurs the Spanish legends to its reeds,
And thou wilt shine in them thyself one day,

PHILIP II

Like a proud emperor who returns from war
In bright and fine array and with a mien
Both frank and youthful, mingling new-made great-
    ness
With that of older times. Come, let us love
Each other and remember, Carlos . . . Come . . .
    Come . . .
            [*They disappear slowly by the steps in the*
                    background.

CURTAIN.

ACT II

The KING's *apartment. Two doors, one right, the other left. A table loaded with bundles of paper and devotional works. A desk is set against it. A confessional in a corner.*

At the rise of the curtain, PHILIP II, *who has just confessed, gets up, and makes the sign of the cross. His* CONFESSOR *also rises, and they both approach the table.*

THE CONFESSOR FRAY BERNARDO.
The avowal that you made to me at confession, my son, will be accounted to you, not as a sin, but as an honour. Prudence commands you to think more often than not the contrary of your words. That which is kept silent alone matters, since God, alone, understands it. [*A pause,* PHILIP II *sits down.*] He made you as you are in order that you might be his faithful king. [*The* COUNT DE FERIA *brings in the King's correspondence. He places it on the table and goes out.*] The world must be saved in spite of the world. A king would be without power if, with such a duty, he placed limits on his right. [PHILIP II *slowly turns over his correspondence, after having broken the seals.*] In our time, the idea of authority is shaken. That nothing should encroach upon it, not even wisdom, is forgotten. You alone understand that well, while the Holy Father values it but little.

PHILIP II.
He does not know what Spain needs.

PHILIP II

Fray Bernardo.

At Rome, they are divided; they grow slack, they
argue. The atmosphere is bad there, and the Pope
breathes it. Now, he who reasons compromises. He
who discusses, weakens. You must believe, affirm,
act.

> [*Suddenly the* King *seizes a letter, from
> which he does not take his eyes. Although
> his* Confessor *becomes more and more
> worked up, he pays scarcely any further
> attention to what he says. His hand
> slowly clenches.*

Such is my faith, the only lofty one;
The only faith that is as pure as fire,
In this moment of time when human justice
Is divorced shamefully from that of God.
England is lost. The Church is, in our Flanders,
Deep-sunken in the mire of wickedness
And sects. The Holy Empire is devoured
By a thousand errors. Darkness tarnishes
The golden sceptre of the emperors.
Europe is seized with frenzy and with madness;
Peoples and kings no longer fear remorse;
And it would seem that all the howling north
    winds
Are Satan's and let loose apostasy.

> [*Becoming calmer and watching the* King *at
> his reading.*

Happily, there is in the universe one Spain, yours.
The war with the Moors has for centuries uplifted
it. It fears neither blood nor punishments. No
summit, however lofty, escapes its inquisitors. You
have burnt, Sire, Carlos de Sesse and his wife Isabelle,
who descended from King Pedro. You overthrew
Domingo de Rojas, of the family of the Posa. A
Cristoval d'Ocampo was killed and his body de-

PHILIP II

livered to the flames. As for the Marchioness d'Amboise . . .

> [*At the sound of the word Amboise, the* KING *instinctively, by a sudden movement of dissimulation, hides the letter which he holds in his hand. His* CONFESSOR *looks at him fixedly.* PHILIP II *perceives this. After a moment's reflection he hands him the letter.*]

PHILIP II.
Read, father. [*At a call of* PHILIP II, *the* DUKE DE FERIA *enters.* PHILIP II *speaks to him in a low voice.*] Duke, go yourself and seek out the Countess de Clermont; bring her here to us.

FRAY BERNARDO. [*Who has only paid attention to his reading.*]
There are in this adventure at least two guilty persons: Don Juan, who allowed the Marchioness d'Amboise to embark, and the Countess de Clermont, mistress of Don Carlos. [*Re-reading the letter.*] Don Juan is not to be relied on. Remember the day on which he left, without orders, to give battle at a distance. His duty was to watch the coasts, and to seize the Marchioness. He has failed in it. Arrest him.

PHILIP II.
Pirates were threatening Corunna. I myself commanded Don Juan to lead my ships and my soldiers there. The coast of Guipuzcoa was free, not by his order, but by mine.

FRAY BERNARDO.
Yet a woman, however clever she may be, cannot

204

PHILIP II

carry out alone so perilous an enterprise, and Don
Juan . . .

PHILIP II.
Do not insist, father.

FRAY BERNARDO. [*Re-reading the report.*]
It is true the report only accuses the countess. Ruy
d'Almedo recognized two of her men-servants as
they arrived in the evening at Renteria. Another
witness holds that the first of the two belonged to
Don Carlos. An inquiry must be ordered.

PHILIP II.
We will examine the Countess de Clermont.

FRAY BERNARDO.
She can baffle interrogation. The Valois find in her
a most precious aid; she is maid of honour, and . . .

PHILIP II. [*In a low voice.*]
A spy . . . I know . . . I know . . .

FRAY BERNARDO.
Don Carlos loves her. She resembles the queen,
your consort. Both come from France; they might
be sisters.

PHILIP II. [*Irritated.*]
I know. I know.

FRAY BERNARDO.
The countess has a firm hold on the heart of Don
Carlos; the love of a prince flatters her woman's
vanity. Don Carlos listens to none but her. The
inquisitors have noticed it, and they are watching
him. His pride, as much as his weakness, makes

them uneasy. If he were not your son. . . . [*Suddenly.*]
Perhaps it was he, Infante of Spain, who saved the
marchioness?

PHILIP II.
Madness!

FRAY BERNARDO.
Don Carlos is dangerous. There can be no certainty . . . he might have . . .

PHILIP II.
Madness, I tell you. . . .

FRAY BERNARDO.
A new man is awakening in him. His health is returning to him; disquieting ideas besiege him. He
expects too much.

PHILIP II.
Don Carlos is only strong by a woman. It is she
who must be put away.

FRAY BERNARDO.
May I, Sire, as I did a little while ago at confession,
tell you my whole thought?

PHILIP II.
I guess it. [*Approaching* FRAY BERNARDO, *and
speaking to him eye to eye.*] Yes, Don Carlos hates
me; yes, Don Carlos is overwrought, blind and
mistaken; yes, Don Carlos must have known the
crime of the Countess; but that Don Carlos, although rash and perhaps dangerous, is none the less
the future King of Spain, who cannot think of betraying me without ruining himself, who, in short,
whatever he may dream, will always respect in my

PHILIP II

person that absolute power which he incarnates as
well as I. We are a same thought of God. If he
forgot it. . . .

FRAY BERNARDO.
May Heaven hear you!

PHILIP II.
And, now, let all this be said, as I confessed my
sins to you a while ago, from me to you, before
Eternity. [*A long pause.*] Take your place here,
father. [*He indicates a desk, left.*] The countess is
coming. The Duke de Feria has gone to fetch
her. You will examine her, and take note of her
answers; and we will communicate them to the
Holy Office.
> [*The* COUNTESS *is brought in by the* DUKE
> DE FERIA, *who thereupon takes his
> place, standing, at the* KING's *right.*

THE COUNTESS. [*To* PHILIP II, *pointing to the* DUKE
and to FRAY BERNARDO.]
Sire, so many judges confuse and frighten me. And
really I do not know. . . .

PHILIP II.
Let all fear be banished from your mind, madam.
My presence should dispel it.

THE COUNTESS.
I came in answer to your call. What I may tell you
concerns your son alone.

PHILIP II. [*To* FRAY BERNARDO.]
Examine the lady.

PHILIP II

FRAY BERNARDO.
The Marchioness d'Amboise has left Spain without
the King's orders. It is you, Madam, who saved
her.

THE COUNTESS. [*Firmly.*]
The marchioness and I were friends. She came of
her own free will to Spain; she could as freely
leave it.

FRAY BERNARDO.
None can, without orders, enter or quit the kingdom.
When the marchioness came from France, she was
a catholic, and we welcomed her. She became a
heretic here with us, and our justice should have
dealt with her. You could not have been ignorant
of this.

THE COUNTESS.
The marchioness has not, so far as I know, abjured
her faith.

FRAY BERNARDO. [*Rudely.*]
That is not true.

THE COUNTESS. [*Turning to the* KING.]
Sire . . . the hostility of your confessor alarms me
. . . I do not know . . .

PHILIP II.
I am studying your embarrassment and your confusion, madam. I read in your attitude what you
are hiding from us.

THE COUNTESS.
But . . .

PHILIP II

FRAY BERNARDO.
Queen Catharine of France sent you among us
knowingly. You serve her here better than any-
body.

THE COUNTESS.
But, Sire, . . .

FRAY BERNARDO.
Your intelligence is keen, and is attracted by secrets.
Where others but look, you watch. Your letters,
yes, your letters, keep France informed of what the
King alone would know.

THE COUNTESS. [*Turning to the* KING.]
I act without deceit, and I think aloud, Sire. At
your court, I am one of the companions and maids
of the queen; I am nothing more. My friendship
for the Marchioness d'Amboise I have displayed
openly. Let it be my ruin, if your laws demand it.
But as for the vile and guilty letters I am supposed
to have written. . . .

PHILIP II.
My suspicions never lead me astray.

THE COUNTESS.
I am defending my honour before you. I swear to
you that I have never written a line that you might
not have read. I limit my defence to that oath.

FRAY BERNARDO.
You would not be the brilliant Countess de Clermont, sought out by the queen, nor the clever
seductive mistress distinguished by a prince, if you
were not guilty . . .

PHILIP II

THE COUNTESS. [*Turning to the* KING.]
You are allowing me to be browbeaten and I am
defenceless, Sire, and you are a nobleman.

PHILIP. [*Sourly.*]
Madam . . .

THE COUNTESS. [*Addressing the* KING *only.*]
Don Carlos chose me, and he loves me. I am giving
him the most precious thing I have: my life. I am
giving it to him wholly. If I were the intriguer you
say, he would not accept me.

FRAY BERNARDO.
Don Carlos is blind because he loves you.

THE COUNTESS. [*To* FRAY BERNARDO.]
You know as well as I his violent past,
The days he spent in weariness and rage;
But you do not know how a mere trifle soothes him.
My heart has never lied, my hand weighed heavy,
And when I met him for the first time, he
It was who came of his own will to me.
My memory retains his sweetest word,
And at this moment, while you torture me,
With cunning, cutting speech,
It still consoles me.
                    [*A silence: the* KING *seems to wait.*
          Sire,
I have an ardent fondness for the Infante;
I love the changing temper of his mind,
Now sad and now triumphant. What care I
For the excesses of his biting hatreds
And his depressions and his childish furies.
I love him as he is, and I am proud
He loves me. I do not inquire how much
My love is sometimes kin to pity, how . . .

PHILIP II

PHILIP II. [*Suddenly severe.*]
It is an insult to my son to love him thus.

THE COUNTESS. [*Indignantly.*]
Oh! Sire, Sire.

PHILIP II.
Keep calm, madam, and answer better.

THE COUNTESS.
I can no longer answer; I see myself surrounded
by snares; you twist my simplest thoughts. If I
give to Don Carlos my attentive and obedient
affection,
I show him, too, the courage that kings need.
I make him greater and I win him over
To the fine pride of being conscious
That he is Infante of Spain,
Of having faith and confidence in himself,
                              [*The* KING *acquiesces.*
Of being one who wills, who learns and judges,
Who finds his right and refuge in his power,
And who, in short, discovers in himself,
After a space of twenty years of loathing,
A heart in keeping with his present dreams.

PHILIP II.
I alone and the men chosen by me form the heart
and mind of a future King of Spain. You are a
foreigner and you are dangerous; your counsels,
your cleverness, your love, are all pernicious.

THE COUNTESS. [*Indignantly.*]
Oh!

PHILIP II.
God alone knows into what errors you are leading

him, and what you tell him at night when you
believe me absent.   The heretics whom you save
between you . . .

THE COUNTESS. [*As though taken by surprise.*]
No, no, your son knew nothing . . .

PHILIP II.
It was you alone, then?

THE COUNTESS.
Well then, yes, I alone am guilty.   I knew what I
was exposing myself to.

PHILIP II. [*To* FRAY BERNARDO, *who is recording.*]
That is the confession.

THE COUNTESS.
And I am not ashamed of it.   My conscience . . .

PHILIP II.
Enough, madam.   To save a friend is nothing when
I remember what you do every day, what you are
really here, a spy.

THE COUNTESS.
I deny it, I deny it.

PHILIP II.
To deny is nothing when I affirm.

THE COUNTESS.
Never! Never!

FRAY BERNARDO.
We have the proofs; we will show them to you;
but confess first of all.

PHILIP II

THE COUNTESS.
It is not true. It cannot be.

FRAY BERNARDO.
Confession is redeeming; it wipes out the sin; it
gains heaven for you. Confess.

THE COUNTESS.
No! No!

FRAY BERNARDO.
Confess, since salvation lies therein.

THE COUNTESS.
No! No!

FRAY BERNARDO.
Since the King knows all.

THE COUNTESS.
No! No!

FRAY BERNARDO.
Since the King so orders.

THE COUNTESS.
No! No! Never! Never!

FRAY BERNARDO. [*Rising.*]
You confessed a moment ago. You will confess
again.
> [*At this moment a violent commotion is heard
> at the door.* DON CARLOS, *with bran-
> dished sword and brushing aside the
> KING's guard, appears.*

DON CARLOS. [*On the threshold.*]
I wish to pass, I wish to see the king, I tell you.

PHILIP II

PHILIP II.
Carlos!

DON CARLOS.
        I wish to speak alone, alone
And without witnesses, to Philip, King
Of Spain, concerning the regard my greatness
Merits, the which is slighted and which he
Neglects.

PHILIP II. [*To* DON CARLOS.]
        Withdraw.

DON CARLOS.   No, never!

THE COUNT DE FERIA.   You forget
That you are in the council-chamber where . . .

DON CARLOS. [*Pointing to the* KING.]
I am here, with him, my father;
I am firm fixed from head to foot;
And I remain. No human force,
Since I have come, will make me go away.
        [*To the* DUKE DE FERIA *and* FRAY BER-
            NARDO *who are watching anxiously*
            DON CARLOS's *sword.*
You need not fear; the king is in no danger.
        [*He throws his sword on to the table.*
Before I left, I muzzled up my hatred.

PHILIP II. [*To* DON CARLOS.]
Speak.

PHILIP II

DON CARLOS. [*Pointing to the* DUKE *and* FRAY
BERNARDO.]
    I will speak when they have gone.
    [*On a sign from* PHILIP II, *the* DUKE *and*
    FRAY BERNARDO *disappear by the door*
    on the right. The DUKE, *without* DON
    CARLOS's *seeing him, carries off the*
    sword. As soon as they have gone, DON
    CARLOS *goes towards the* COUNTESS,.
    and taking her by the hand.
Oh! do not follow them, madam, but pass this way.
[*He leads her to the door on the left.*] I love the Countess
de Clermont. Such is my pleasure. A short while
back, the Duke de Feria came and tore her away
from my apartments while I was praying in the
oratory. He brought her by force to you: why?

PHILIP II.
I am not of those who may be questioned.

DON CARLOS.
My heart is full and eaten up with cares.
I wish to know in short what rights a duke . . .

PHILIP II.
That tone of boldness and defiance you
Must cease, my son, and listen to me calmly,
As you were wont to do. Nought has been done
That should displease you; I am certain too
That you will understand me, if you hear me.
The Princes of Lorraine are soliciting you in mar-
riage, you, Infante of Spain, for their niece Mary,.
who was Queen of France. Your choice might
already have rested on the Archduchess Anne of
Austria, or Marguerite, princess of the house of
Valois. I have formed for you up to the present no-

215

PHILIP II

project which would clash with a preference. I fear
but one thing: the vexation of the Countess de
Clermont. That is why I questioned her.

DON CARLOS.
A prince of my blood loves countesses but espouses
queens. The countess will approve me on the day
I marry. But I am young, and my affection would
remain free for some time yet.

PHILIP II.
Think that at your age I had chosen a queen.

DON CARLOS.
Neither Marguerite de Valois nor this Mary of
Scotland, who, they say, is adventurous and beau-
tiful, attracts me so much as the simple princess of
Germany.

PHILIP II.
This choice pleases me still more than all the others.
Quite enough ties unite us to the Valois. It is to
the Empire that we must turn. [*Kindly.*] What if
your union restored to us the crown of Charles V!

DON CARLOS.
Oh! if that dream can ever come to pass,
It will fulfil the fondest of my hopes;
And I shall be the holy emperor
Who symbolizes human might and power,
And in the world's name speaks aloud to God.
I shall march armed from wonder on to wonder;
And Europe will at length have found the man
Who, after a thousand years of fruitless efforts,
Will wrest the tomb where sleeps Christ's memory
From those who shut it off a Christian's guard.

216

PHILIP II

PHILIP II.
Your blood indeed is hot and virile: madness,
Love, conquest, glory—all their many perils!
But we are of one mind, and I am happy.
What if they saw us, those who rack their minds
To break in us the bonds made fast by God!
I wish thee bold and great. Here is my hand.

DON CARLOS. [*Hesitating.*]
Father!

PHILIP II.
        Not that which strikes and twists and prisons,
But that which smoothed thy fiery, fevered brow
When thou wert but my sad Infante.

DON CARLOS. [*Holding back.*]   We
Are so far each from the other.

PHILIP II.   I insist.
                [DON CARLOS *gives him his hand.*
    The archduchess will bring her sober virtues
into our court. She speaks of you and admires you;
she loves you already. Our ambassador keeps me
informed.

DON CARLOS.
So little is needed to win me. I await this gentle
child as a friend who will understand my humours
and my angers; and I shall be discreetly touched
by the knowledge, without telling her so.

PHILIP II.
Happy princess!

PHILIP II

DON CARLOS.
And then, she will be, after the Queen, the highest
among women. She will be surrounded with stately
homage, and her presence will make the court
young again. I shall be proud for her sake of being
a majesty; and we will govern together a distant
province of our kingdoms; we . . .

PHILIP II. [*Interrupting.*]
The Countess de Clermont will astonish her perhaps; but the Queens of Spain must be indulgent;
they have always been so. Besides, the Countess
wins over even those who are at first hostile to her.
Just now, we were talking together of her friends,
of France. We even spoke at some length about you.
> [*During this time* DON CARLOS *walks up
> and down the room, and stops without
> at first taking notice of it, before the desk
> where* FRAY BERNARDO, *in his hurry,
> has left uncovered the interrogatory of
> the* COUNTESS.

DON CARLOS. [*Confidingly.*]
Sir, you would love her if you knew her well.
She stirs me up or curbs me, at her will.
I feel she is devoted to me, kind
And needful for the work I meditate,
With which one day my valour and my ardour
Will enrich Spain. She is my fresh-found health.
On new roads she escorts my trembling feet.
If I dared, I would even speak to you
Of her with tender, violent, deep-felt words.

PHILIP II.
But why fear, in this most beneficent hour,
When we are to each other as before,

218

PHILIP II

A father proud to see his son's quick life,
To hear him dream his destiny on earth,
To mould the future for him. . . .

> [Don Carlos *for some moments past has
> been gazing fixedly at the interrogatory
> before his eyes. Suddenly, tearing it
> with clenched hand.*

Don Carlos.   Ah! my father,
In truth, it is enough to make me doubt
Heaven's thunder! What, here in this very room,
While you entice with crafty, crooked words
The admirable woman whom I love
The procurators of the Holy Office
Record beneath those eyes [*He points to the* King.]
     her downfall and
Her sentence.

Philip II.
Carlos!

Don Carlos.
          You dared to speak of her,
You dared to name her in one breath with me,
And the name did not freeze your lips with fear,
Nor did you tremble that you were so vile!

Philip II. [*Rising.*]
Silence, Infante, you insult in me . . .

Don Carlos. [*Exasperated.*]
So much the better. Ah! So much the better!
Always you have surrounded me with plots;
Your words to me are like a bunch of black
And poisonous, wreathing snakes, that all combine

219

PHILIP II

To fascinate at first, and, after, crush.
Evil attains in you to such excess
That when I think of evil it is you
I think of, you, my father. If I come
Some day to rule, I shall forget all else,
Except the horror that I have of you,
And the dull anger that I am your blood.

PHILIP II. [*Shaken.*]
My son, my son.
              [*He makes for the prie-dieu, as though
              tottering, and falls down before it.*

DON CARLOS. [*Coming up to him.*]
                    Not so; I spurn you; I
No longer wish to be your son. You are
A knavish king, no more, who must be punished,
And who dishonours in himself, his sons
And his ancestors. This your reign will be
The terror of the future. Here in Spain,
You are hated, and in Flanders, you are cursed.
Your base and shameful power must be taken.
I feel a dark scheme germinate within me;
The chrism with which your temples were anointed
Has been wiped out, and you may clasp your hands
And thank your God that I am now disarmed.
              [*He goes out backward, looking for his sword.*

PHILIP II. [*With pain.*]
Unhappy man, unhappy man. The thought
Of murder crossed his brain; and he desires,
O God! my downfall and my death. By what
Most criminal intent his life has been
Sustained! By what mad, frightful, bloody hope!
If I could find within his seething brain
One paramount excuse for his foul sin,

PHILIP II

It would be different; but he has attacked
Spain and himself, and that which sums them up,
My power, me! O God, who mete out strength
To kings in due proportion, stay in me
Their heart that weeps and dreads his mortal hatred;
Wipe out all human weakness in me that
My rights may be maintained intact and sovereign.

A GUARD. [*Entering.*]
My lord Don Juan.

PHILIP II.
Let him wait. [*Changing his mind.*] Eh no! let him
enter.

DON JUAN. [*Agitated.*]
Sire . . .

PHILIP II. [*Calmly.*]
What then?

DON JUAN.
Don Carlos has shut himself up in his apartments.
He will see nobody. Just now, he ran through the
palace with staring eyes and threatening fists . . .

PHILIP II.
We have been talking together like good friends.
We even shook hands together. I do not know what
has upset him. He confides in you; tell me about
him.

DON JUAN.
Ah! Sire, if you only knew how much his inaction
weighs upon him, how dull in this palace are the
days on which he wanders aimlessly, and despairs at
length.

PHILIP II

PHILIP II.
But the countess, and her beauty, and their love?

DON JUAN.
Love was to him the lovely hand of joy,
Indeed! that tore him like a sudden prey
From the unhealthy, tragic, feverish dullness;
And he was cured. He breathed the scents of all
Affection's flowers; he was happy; now
That love impels him to desire still more;
He dreams of being a bold and fiery captain.

PHILIP II.
Longings for love and glory—both the same!

DON JUAN.
Sire, since his future lies in your sole hands,
Since he still craves what he has ever craved,
Since he has only this one prayer . . .

PHILIP II.
I understand. But the government of Flanders is
promised to the Duke of Alva. My word is given.

DON JUAN.
Everything is settled or unsettled according to your
wisdom.

PHILIP II.
But our northern provinces are unsubdued. To
vanquish them, terror and a cool head are needed.
Sieges of towns, assaults, battles, the rough and
tiring life of camps. Don Carlos could not manage it.

DON JUAN.
I should be at his side; I would put my courage to
the service of his; I can command and conquer.
Where old captains fail, the young triumph.

222

P'HILIP II

PHILIP II.

I have had transported to Lombardy by Don Garcia all the infantry that occupied Naples, Sicily, and Sardinia. I have ordered the Duke of Albuquerque to divide into two the number of my cavalry at Milan. All these troops and those I am raising in Germany know, like and have confidence in Alvarez of Toledo. They know that he is to command them and lead them to Flanders. My sister herself, who fears the duke, has come to understand that he alone can help and save her there. All these difficult measures have been taken and agreed to, and you would have me upset them for a child's caprice?

DON JUAN.

But this child's caprice may overthrow both the throne and Spain.

PHILIP II.

What do you mean?

DON JUAN.

I love Don Carlos, Sire, more than myself;
But you I duly serve, and you for me
Represent the supreme authority
That none shall break. I tremble both for you
And him; I dread the excess of his strange nature,
His heart that, overcast and overwrought,
By turns, is held in check by no restraint
If it conceive a wish. His uncurbed soul
Is mad and monstrous in its vengeances.

PHILIP II. [*Very calmly.*]

I know, Don Juan; my son intends my death.

223

PHILIP II

DON JUAN.
Oh! Sire, what a suspicion! Never a thought
Or such design! . . . His heart is filled with too
Great a respect.

PHILIP II.   But what does he desire then?

DON JUAN.
I have told you, to go to Flanders, to rule it in your
name for the good of Spain. He remembers that at
his age, under Charles V, you were master there;
that the hand of his grandfather was less tight than
yours. And this thought haunts him, pursues him
day and night, and dazzles him to such an extent
that it blinds him. He becomes overwrought, feverish, hallucinated. Ah! Sire, I appeal to your wisdom;
everything may yet be put right and in order; but
I pray you to save Don Carlos from the peril. . . .

PHILIP II.
What peril?

DON JUAN.
I hesitate. I do not know whether I should tell
you. . . . Do you pardon him?

PHILIP II.
Am I not his father?

DON JUAN.
But it is still more than pardon; it is your assistance
that I implore.

PHILIP II.
Are we not two brothers who love a same child?
Have we not learned to know him in order to

224

PHILIP II

overlook all his caprices, even if some madness filled
his brain? I do not know, but we might consider
together whether something could be done.

DON JUAN.
But suppose his dream were so mad . . .

PHILIP II.
Never mind the dream. As the peccadillo of a
prince, it is absolved beforehand . . .

DON JUAN.
Then you promise . . .

PHILIP II.
Better still, I reassure you . . .

DON JUAN.
Well then, he wishes suddenly to flee,
And make for France, where certain lords have
    sworn
To serve him, all together, faithfully.
Berghes and Montigny only feigned to be
Your counsellors; they tempted him; they poured
Out false and corrupt advice to him; they threw
Pitch on his fiery soul; and others came
Promising armies to support his cause
And lead his pride through all the towns of Flanders.

PHILIP II. [*After a secret astonishment.*]
Thus his mad rage for money is explained,
The sudden loans he has contracted in
Toledo, Leon, Burgos and Medina:
Everything tallies and falls into place
Exactly. When shall I suspect enough?

PHILIP II

DON JUAN.
Ah Sire!

PHILIP II.
> The knots of such a plot must have
Been tied most noiselessly. The enterprise
Appeals to him, and so Don Carlos listens.

DON JUAN. [*Anxiously.*]
Sire! Sire!

PHILIP II. [*Having recovered.*]
> Let not your heart misdoubt me; Carlos
Is brave and wild; his boldness pleases me.
> > [*With a slight irony.*
If now I did not hasten to appoint
This prince as ruler of my provinces,
His courage, though so young, would take them
> from me.   [*A silence; then suddenly.*
Well then! I give them to him; tell him so,
And that henceforth his father will watch over
His destinies.

DON JUAN.   May I believe you, Sire?

PHILIP II.
Indeed, your only fault was not to have dared
To bring the matter home to me more closely.
You must not be mistrustful of me.

DON JUAN.   Thanks!
You gain Don Juan and Don Carlos thus.
I fly to promise him what you have promised.
How right I was to come without delay
And confide in you who remain the master,
So saving Carlos by doing my duty.
> [*He goes out.* PHILIP II *rises and goes to-
> wards the door.*
226

PHILIP II

PHILIP II. [*At the door on the left.*]
Let my notary, Don Pedro de Hoyos, be brought
here immediately. [*At the door on the right, calling.*]
Fray Bernardo! Fray Hieronimo! [*They appear. To*
FRAY BERNARDO.] Father, I was mistaken. I spoke
thoughtlessly just now of Don Carlos's crime. Now,
I know—I have the proof of it—that he encouraged
and arranged the flight of the Marchioness d'Amboise.
The real criminal is he; the Countess is only an
accomplice.

FRAY BERNARDO. [*Looking fixedly at the* KING.]
Yet . . .

PHILIP II.
His punishment will be tragic and prompt, I swear it.

FRAY BERNARDO.
And the trial of the countess whose confession we
hold . . .

PHILIP II.
What matters a countess of France, when a prince
of Spain is in question! Don Carlos will be judged
this night. And the Holy Father and Europe will
know that Philip never hesitates, even against himself, to safeguard the rights of God.

FRAY BERNARDO.
Such an example is the highest that you can offer.

PHILIP II.
You will help me, Father. Since such is your right,
you will replace the inquisitor general, Don Diego
d'Espinoza. You will appoint four judges as your
assistants; they will be informed by you of the

horror I have of this crime. Don Carlos, being ill, will not appear at the trial; he will be represented by Martin de Valesco, doctor of the councils of Castile, and by me. I will defend him to the best of my ability. Thus, everything will be done according to rules, secretly, but suddenly. [DON PEDRO DE HOYOS *enters. The* MONKS *make to withdraw.* PHILIP II *motions them to stay. To the* MONKS.] Stay: you will be my witnesses. [*To* DON PEDRO.] Sit, and take down what I shall tell you. I, the King, being present Fray Bernardo, bishop of Cuenca, my confessor, and Fray Hieronimo, of the order of Saint Francis, attest that, in promising Don Juan of Austria to nominate Don Carlos governor of my States of Flanders and to authorize the said Don Juan to conduct him thither, I acted neither freely nor of my own full will, but solely to avoid greater evils and to protect from peril as much my life as the honour of my crown. Let none therefore take advantage of my promises. [*To the witnesses,* FRAY BERNARDO *and* HIERONIMO.] I will sign first; you after. [*While the* KING *signs, the curtain falls.*]

ACT III

The COUNTESS'S *apartment. On the right, the alcove;
in the background, a large window. On the left,
two doors. Night.*

DON CARLOS.

FOR the first time, I have defied my father;
I held him at my mercy; and my anger
Intimidated him and filled his heart
With fright. He felt death threaten him through me.
He trembled, prayed; and I no longer fear.

                              [*To the* COUNTESS.

To think that he spoke to me of thee with quiet
words, that he enticed me towards him, that he
dreamed of me as emperor, that he imposed on me
with affection. . . . Ah! beloved, why wert thou
not present when I branded him!

THE COUNTESS.
He will never . . . never forget.

DON CARLOS.
Let him remember!
I alone in this palace
Hold in my hands
An equal right to his—and the future!
Since his race cannot finish in himself,
Since the heavens will it so,
Nobody in the world,
The King especially, can set aside,

PHILIP II

In the mingled glory and darkness of its reign,
The divine order that I carry on.
            [*A pause; taking the* COUNTESS's *hand.*
What didst thou say to the monk?

THE COUNTESS.
The truth. They challenged my sincerity; and I
was sincere to the last limit: I have brought about
my downfall. The Holy Office is no doubt already
examining my case and condemning me. Perhaps,
by and by, its emissaries will seek me out even here.
The King knows now that I saved the marchioness,
that I alone . . .

DON CARLOS.
Unhappy woman, why didst thou not name me first?

THE COUNTESS.
Not one of his suspicions must be made
To fall upon his son.

DON CARLOS.   But I say he fears me.
I have cowed, vanquished him, Philip the king;
Never have I felt such pride swell up in me,
Nor for my enterprise so bright an omen.

THE COUNTESS.
Carlos, if thou didst but know what insults he heaped
upon me! What suspicions he brought to bear on
me! I, Countess de Clermont, was accused of spying
on the Court, the King, the Queen, thyself.

DON CARLOS.
Thou art ignorant of Spanish affairs. Those of
Flanders alone . . .

PHILIP II

THE COUNTESS.
Ah! those are thy glory and thy life! . . .

DON CARLOS. [*Pressing her to him.*]
Besides, what the King thinks or says,
What matters it to us when it is I
Alone who climb, when my impatience counts
Off one by one the all too numerous moments
That still delay my coming into Flanders
With all my golden trumpets. I defend,
Protect and bear thee with me. I pour out
For thee the intrepid ardour that, when I
Was burdened with a sluggish mournfulness,
Thou didst instil into my weary heart.
My youth won over to thee now escorts thee;
And, in my turn, I save and kindle thee;
           [CARLOS, *as though intoxicated, leans his*
               head on the COUNTESS'S *shoulder.*

THE COUNTESS. [*Maternally.*]
Cradle in my arms thy fever and thy triumph,
O King! Hope and be happy with thy passion;
Taste the voluptuousness of thy desires;
Forget thy mournful past, and take thy dreams
For a real world a god has made for thee.
I love thee too much in this joyous hour
To turn thee from it or to change thy mind.
Thou singest of thyself as conqueror
And lord of all the earth with words that spring
From the depths of thy happiness; and even if
To-morrow it should vanish, yet to-day
Its joy and light illuminate thy head.
And at this moment that thought is enough. . . .
           [*Going towards a seat near the window, as*
               if to rest CARLOS, *who yields.*
Repose in thy illusion, quietly;
To-morrow thy bare head will brunt the tempest.

231

PHILIP II

DON JUAN. [*Knocks at the door and enters familiarly.*
DON CARLOS, *seeing him enter, frees himself but
slightly from the arms of the* COUNTESS.]
All that I promised, Carlos, I will keep.
Myself, with my bright vessels, will conduct
Thy youth across the seas to Flanders, where
Its peoples will acclaim our passage through
Their cities with a shouting of deliverance.
Their privileges will spring up once again;
And thou wilt be the sovereign lord and master
Of the fine country that commands the North
And looks towards France. Thy hour has come.

DON CARLOS.   And who
Assured thee so?

DON JUAN.   The King.

THE COUNTESS.   I am afraid.

DON CARLOS.
How I must have subdued and cowed him that
He gives way suddenly to such a choice!

DON JUAN.
What decided him, was to see thee spring to life
again: to see thy youth, thy courage, thy boldness;
and to know with what impatience thou dost direct,
and, if need be, command, for thy glory.
I told him . . .

DON CARLOS.
Thou didst well to tell him . . .

THE COUNTESS. [*Frightened.*]
Don Juan!

PHILIP II

DON JUAN.
Oh! be without fear, madam. I sounded the King
before venturing. I acted with prudence only after
the King had already promised.

DON CARLOS.
It was needless. He fears me. He will grant me
everything.

DON JUAN.
He had given his word to the Duke of Alva. His
cavalry in Lombardy and his troops in Naples and
Sicily were ready. His sister, the Regent, after a
thousand objections, had yielded to his arguments;
she had become resigned to welcoming the duke.
But what matters! He prefers to satisfy his peoples
and his son.

THE COUNTESS.
When did this change take place?

DON JUAN.   A moment since.

THE COUNTESS.
How strange it seems, and such a doubt grows in me
That I cannot believe it true.

DON JUAN.   Eh! countess, why
Do you suspect the King so violently?
Am I of those who are duped, and Philip, my brother,
Has he no longer, then, the royal right
Of being sincere? I am a man who counts,
And who is not to be imposed on, I . . .

DON CARLOS.
Tell me, Don Juan, when shall we arrive in Flanders?

233

PHILIP II

DON JUAN.
The King will arrange that himself.

DON CARLOS.
On what date?

DON JUAN.
Eh, what matters!

DON CARLOS.
Not so! I will no longer submit to the good pleasure of the King.

DON JUAN.
I have his promise.

DON CARLOS.
I have my obligations. A hundred and fifty thousand ducats swell my coffers, and letters of credit reach me from Seville. My gentlemen-in-waiting distribute them, and the Count de Guelves and Juan Nunes are my sureties.

DON JUAN.
But thou surely dost not require that Philip should recall forthwith the Duke of Alva? Whatever his will and his power, he cannot . . .

DON CARLOS.
Then I will act alone.

DON JUAN.   But that is madness!
A line of kings all bind thee to thy fate.
I hear thy grandsire's voice ascending towards thee.

DON CARLOS.
I will hear nothing; I will start alone.

PHILIP II

THE COUNTESS.
Yes! Yes!

DON JUAN.
    Oh! what disasters does thy madness
Forebode. Once more I venture to beseech thee,
By all that re-awakens our old friendship,
Kept intact round the memories of our childhood,
Not to oppose the action of the King.
I would not have thee, Carlos, start without me,
Nor my tried valiancy abandon thine;
I wish to be at hand in all devotion
To ward off or forestall ill-chance's blows.
The King is in the mood to grant us all;
His own youth flits before him; and he loves thee;
He now awaits fulfilment of his plans,
And then together we will conquer.

DON CARLOS.   Well,
I have decided; he shall have two days.
Good-bye, Don Juan!   [DON JUAN *goes out.*

THE COUNTESS.   Carlos, I am afraid.
Philip is full of craft and false pretence;
What if he is deluding you with hope
While he prepares his blow in darkness?

DON CARLOS.   He could not,
So sure my victory is, my flight so certain.
With or without my father, no matter how,
I will accomplish all that I have said,
Magnificently. Don Juan will escort me,
Like a proud captain, for he loves me, while
He does not love the King. His noble heart
Will be unable to resist the flow
Of my good-fortune, that will carry him

235

Grandly and amply on its swelling tide.
My soul has never felt a mood so golden. . . .
                    [*He approaches the* COUNTESS.
Give me thy fingers, thy hands, thy brow, thine eyes!
Open the golden garden of thy hair
Where gleams of light and perfumes waft and move.
                    [*He unbinds the* COUNTESS's *hair.*
Give me thy lips to my lips, thy red lips,
So that my mouth, child, may devour their fire.
          [*He kisses her madly, then makes to go away.*
          She holds him more tightly.

THE COUNTESS.
Let us remain here a long, long time yet.
I am afraid, I know not why, of this
Swift dawn, lined with black bars at the horizon.
Tell me again thy heart is mine, that I
Am right to sink and lose myself in thee.

DON CARLOS. [*As though praying.*]
It is only thy voice that I would hear
During eternity;
It is only in thine eyes and their calm gaze
My wild desires
Would sink and rest
During eternity;
And it is only in thy deep soul
That I would withdraw from the world
During eternity.

THE COUNTESS. [*Passionately.*]
Again! Again!

DON CARLOS. [*Folding the* COUNTESS *in his arms.*]
          Thou art for me the Virgin,
Triumphant 'mid the golden forests of tapers,

PHILIP II

That for a hundred years has been invoked
At Guadeloupe; thou art for me the strength,
The fervour and the dazzling happiness
That flows within my arteries with my blood;
Thou art for me the rapture and the splendour
By which the earth lives, and I feel unworthy
And most unfortunate that, by a dark
And voluntary torment,
I have not yet been able
To win thee in the eyes of heaven:
I wish to suffer to deserve our gladness!

THE COUNTESS.
Ah! what mad dream art thou a prey to now!
Love, youthful love, friend, like a torrent leaps
In countries radiating so with flame
That they absorb the shadow made by death.
When we are both in Flanders and our fate
Has set our souls alight with other thoughts,
And burns our hearts with a more resolute fire,
We will love love for love's sake and no more.
                          [*Noises without.*
DON CARLOS.
Oh! thou wert to me sister, mother, lover;
Thou hast shown me with thy eager, tender hands
Strife and its dangers like a healing power.
Rejoice, for now the far horizons burn
With the golden rays my dreams have thrown upon
     them.
I march with standards and with swords encom-
     passed,
And I am filled with conquering blood to bursting.
My fortune before heaven is renewed,
And all is pride and gladness with new vision:
I am intoxicated with myself.
                     [*Violent noises at the door.*
237

PHILIP II

THE COUNTESS. [*Very agitated.*]
Listen, listen.

DON CARLOS. [*Suddenly decided.*]
        Eh, let them enter!

THE COUNTESS.   Madness!

DON CARLOS. [*Protecting the* COUNTESS.]
I am thy champion, and my soul is filled
So with thy rapture, child, that I would try
A fall with death.

THE COUNTESS.   Carlos, my beloved . . .

DON CARLOS.
I have taken in my hands thy fate; alone
I wish to save thee.

THE COUNTESS.   Carlos! Carlos!

DON CARLOS.   Let
Them enter!
        [DON CARLOS *runs and opens wide the door.*
           FRAY BERNARDO *and his* SOLDIERS *fill*
           the room. They surround DON CARLOS
           rapidly. The MONK *advances and reads.*

FRAY BERNARDO.
        In the name of the Holy Office
And of the Holy Patrimony of
The Church . . .

DON CARLOS. [*Protecting the* COUNTESS.]
        I am Carlos of Spain, monk. I
Forbid thee; do not dare . . .

238

PHILIP II

FRAY BERNARDO.   Forbid to God;
'Tis he alone who speaks here, he who wills.

DON CARLOS.
I am thy King.

FRAY BERNARDO.
                    God is yours, and God speaks
To you. Hear him and hold your peace, Don
          Carlos.   [*A silence.*
Death at this moment opens hell to you.

DON CARLOS. [*Astonished.*]
Hell . . .

FRAY BERNARDO.
          I arrive in time that you may die
In pardon after having suffered long.

DON CARLOS.
To me! me! opens hell to me!

FRAY BERNARDO.   Prince, none surpasses,
However high he be, God's judgments.

DON CARLOS. [*Prostrated.*]   Hell!

FRAY BERNARDO.
In the name of the Holy Office and of the Holy
Patrimony of the Church, Carlos, Prince of the
Asturias, son of Philip, second of the name, has
been declared guilty of having removed, by his help
and succour, the Marchioness d'Amboise, enemy
of the faith and of Spain, from the justice of Rome
and of the King. To testify which, the tribunal of
the Holy Office has condemned him to the penalties

prescribed, which he will undergo without delay,
he being spared, having regard to his rank of Infante,
the garotte and the stake.

DON CARLOS. [*As though stupefied.*]
Hell! to open hell to me! to open . . .

FRAY BERNARDO.
Your thoughts must be devoted to repentance,
Now, Prince of Spain, whom Jesus Christ will
  pardon.
There is no crime so great that cannot be
Wiped out by his forgiveness. Does your heart
Repent its trespass?

DON CARLOS. [*Mechanically.*]
    Yes.

FRAY BERNARDO.   Sincerely?

DON CARLOS.   Yes.

FRAY BERNARDO.
I leave you then to pray.

THE COUNTESS. [*As though awakening.*]
       Oh! dreadful monks!
So 'tis no longer I who am their mark,
No longer I they punish and they kill;
'Tis he, the poor child whom I re-awakened
To life. O heavens whose great justice is
Enslaved by those who call themselves its servants,
O pale and flaming heavens whose vast heights
Become illuminated suddenly

PHILIP II

By shining heroes who were kings on earth,
Do you not hear the voices of despair,
The cries of torture that a Philip of Spain
Tears out of Christian soil?

> [*Bending towards* Don Carlos.
>   O poor Infante,

Who tremblest now! O thou who wert my master!
O sad heart burnt with fever and with schemes!
How proudly thou didst speak but yesterday,
And how abased thou art before a priest!

> [Don Carlos *remains as though dazed.*
>   *The* Countess *advancing towards the*
>   Monk.

Monk, murder me together with King Carlos;
Knowing what he did, I wish to take my part
Entire in what you name his sin and plot.
This is my sole desire, my only prayer;
Our love is of that kind that crosses death.

Fray Bernardo.
King Philip alone is master of your fate.

The Countess.
What do you need then, monk, to strike me now?
Alone I carried out the whole; alone
I stay here to defy you, and, to-night,
To save, when you are sleeping, those you have
Condemned and doomed. The Infante Carlos loved
    me;
And my unwary fervour sowed his heart
With eager seeds: love, strife, revolt and pity
For those whose cries you drown and suffocate
Within your mashing-vats of fire.

Fray Bernardo. [*Coldly.*]   Pray! Pray!

PHILIP II

THE COUNTESS.
No, no! Blood reddens all your pastoral staves;
My faith has vanished, and my greatest torment
Will be that I have not cried out in public:
                    [*She cries aloud.*
I tear my soul from your ferocious dogmas.

FRAY BERNARDO. [*Violently, to the* SOLDIERS.]
Take her away from here, and shackle her.
She is damned.
          [*Some of the* SOLDIERS *seize the* COUNTESS.

DON CARLOS. [*Mechanically and stupidly.*]
          Open hell! To open hell!

FRAY BERNARDO. [*To the* SOLDIERS *who remain and
     pointing to* DON CARLOS.]
Seize him and do what is needful.
          [*The* SOLDIERS *push* DON CARLOS, *who
          struggles, into the alcove, whence a
          great cry is heard. They are strang-
          ling him. While they are killing him
          behind the shut curtains,* FRAY BER-
          NARDO *absolves him.*
Since you have repented, I absolve you from your
former sins, from those which you have committed
with that woman [*he points to the door by which
the* COUNTESS *went out*], from those which you are
committing perhaps in this moment of revolt and
rage. In the name of the Father, Son and Holy
Ghost. Amen.
          [*The* SOLDIERS *re-appear; the body of* DON
          CARLOS *lies in disorder on the bed.*

242

PHILIP II

Stretch him out lengthways.   Place his hands
Crosswise upon his breast.

[To the CAPTAIN OF THE GUARDS.
Go, seek the King.

[At the moment when the word "King" *is
pronounced,* PHILIP II *himself opens the
door nearest the back scene, and appears on the threshold. He advances
slowly towards the bed, and falls on
his knees, his head between his hands.*

CURTAIN

243

HELEN OF SPARTA

A TRAGEDY IN FOUR ACTS

TRANSLATED BY

JETHRO BITHELL

NOTE

*H*ÉLÈNE DE SPARTE was published by the Nouvelle Revue Française in Paris in 1912. The play was produced at the Théâtre du Châtelet, Paris, on May 4th of the same year, the scenery and dresses being designed by Bakst.

TO MY FRIENDS

STEPHAN ZWEIG AND VALÈRE BRUSSOV

WHO TRANSLATED INTO GERMAN AND

RUSSIAN THIS LYRICAL

TRAGEDY

DRAMATIS PERSONAE

HELEN . . . . MMES. IDA RUBINSTEIN
ELECTRA . . . VERA SERGINE
WOMEN, GIRLS, AND CHILDREN.
POLLUX . . . MM. DE MAX
MENELAUS . . . DESJARDINS
CASTOR . . . ROGER KARL
SIMONIDES⎱ *Nobles.*
EUPHORAS⎰
SHEPHERDS, VINE-DRESSERS, COWHERDS.
SOLDIERS.

SCENE

On the Right: The palace of Menelaus, with terrace.
On the Left: A grove of olive trees, with the statue of
                a faun, rustic seats, and a fountain.
In the Centre: An empty space ending in a balustrade
                reached by a flight of stone steps.
In the Background: Forests with roads winding down
                towards the palace.

249

ACT I

Scene I

Pollux, *Shepherds, Cowherds, Vinedressers, Nobles,*
Simonides, Euphoras.

A Shepherd.
I T is true, then:
They have come back!
They are come forth from the forest track
To the tilled fields again.
They breathe our air which is gentle and mild,
And every step they take from the lone
Dark mountains, and the forest wild,
Leads them, with glory crowned, to Sparta and
their own.

A Vinedresser.
They say they have wandered through the length
of winters untold,
Buffeted by the winds, and savagely blown
To Egypt, and then back again to Crete,
From ocean unto ocean rolled;
They say they have seen the ports of cities splendid,
Where vast and crimson gods in beams that beat
Bear the sun and the moon on their brows of gold . . .
But the tales of men, it is true, are never ended. . . .

A Shepherd.
But is it sure indeed
That they who have been seen

HELEN OF SPARTA

Hasting, through festal welcoming,
Along the roads that hither lead,
Are Helen the Queen,
And Menalaus the King?

A VINEDRESSER.
Pollux, at least, doubts, if no others do . . .

A SHEPHERD.
Some swear it; others waver; sniff a plot.

SIMONIDES.
Pollux may well be sad, if this be true.

EUPHORAS.
If Menelaus is King, Pollux is not . . .

SIMONIDES.
The war and Troy, it is an ancient tale . . .
Who shall remember glories growing pale?

EUPHORAS.
For twenty years Pollux the evil-hearted
Has ruled in Sparta with no gentle hand.
Zeus himself made him the tyrant of the land
When Menelaus to ocean perils departed.

A SHEPHERD.
He has been a ruler sage, more just than others.

SIMONIDES.
Your rights he grants you, ours he smothers . . .
The most just are the unjust, in their own despite.

A SHEPHERD.
Quarrels have smouldered out, thanks to his will:
Now cries of hate, complaints, are still,
And grow not, as they did of old, from morn till
    night.

HELEN OF SPARTA

SIMONIDES.
We held our peace and let him have his way,
While war with Ilium raged,
Lest here another warfare should be waged.

EUPHORAS.
But Menelaus and Helen return to-day,
And now all sullen rancour should be driven
By gladness out of hearts that have forgiven.

ANOTHER NOBLE. [*Who had entered some time before.*]
It was a fisherman on the coast, they say,
Who was the first to mark
The long oars and the tall sails of the King's bark,
Like a great dove coming across the foam,
Sailing, in the clear wind, home.
The waves from the west to the east, under the
    showers
Of the sun's rays, were like a garden of flowers.
Menelaus leapt to the shore, leaving Helen on board;
Up from the towns and the fields the people poured,
And received him at first with shouts and with
    peevish snarling, for
Nobody thought he was a hero home from the war.
Suddenly somebody came who knew the King,
As soon as he looked in his face and heard the speech
    of his lip;
And mothers now, that have followed their husbands,
    cling
To the hearts of their long-lost sons returned in the
    ship.
Then came the Queen among them: her eyes
    seemed to be dreaming,
And suddenly all the crowd, with voices tempestu-
    ous and high,

253

HELEN OF SPARTA

Shouted " Helen! Helen!" and the heavens shook
 with the cry,
And the great noise, from the sea-shore streaming,
Spread with its message of sweetness and peace,
Till the echoes of Greece,
And the sea and the shore and the nymph's cove,
And the satyr's grove,
Rang with it, rang with it long, till the evening fell.
These are the tidings a swift-foot runner from Argos
 has come to tell.

SIMONIDES.

No one can doubt any longer that favouring breezes
 have blown
The Atrides and Helen his consort homeward at
 last to their own,
And that now in the mountains yonder his chariot
 is racing along,
Escorted by nobles that gather to welcome them
 throng by throng,
While the people fall on their knees as the car
 races by.

EUPHORAS.

Pollux forthwith sent Castor out to meet them.
Let us prepare a festival to greet them.

POLLUX. [*Enters with a company of slaves bearing
 flowers, fruits, and branches.*]
Wreathe ye this naked terrace stone
With the garlanded glory of all these flowers,
So that their colours may join in our welcome's cry;
And let these roses, heavy and full-blown,
Fall from this lintel in showers;
And round these pillars whitely shining,
And round these martial lances

HELEN OF SPARTA

Reared on high,
See that the woven ivy greenly glances,
With foliage free and tendrils intertwining.
                                [To the cowherds.
And you, among your teeming cattle take
The fattest bulls, to gild their horns; and shake
Mint and viburnum on the highway; and,
Along the paths our rulers' feet shall tread,
Among the white boughs you have scattered, shed
Bright pebbles, and soft luminous sand.
For it is my will that the sea and the winds and the
      woods and the mountain steep,
The running brook and the road where the dust
      lies deep,
It is my will that all things in city and plain
Shall welcome Helen home again.
                        [Swiftly to the shepherds.
Lead to the pastures, and marshal them there by the
      edge of the grass,
Goats, rams, and ewes with fleeces hanging splendid,
So that the King and the Queen may see that their
      herds are well tended,
And gladden their eyes with the thrift of their
      wealth as they pass.   *[Exeunt shepherds.*
The cellars are full, and the meadows are green by
      the streams.
Not for myself but for him I have laboured and
      planned.
With corn the whole country teems;
And shamefaced hunger dare not walk
Where the good grain weighs down the stalk,
To feed the populous cities of the laughing land.

A VINEDRESSER. [*To* POLLUX.]
Although it is the King they acclaim to-day,
Each of us here, in the depths of his thought,

Will remember you who were righteous in your sway,
And sage in counsel, and strong when for the poor
   you fought.

POLLUX.
If you would please me, speak this comfort, friend,
When Helen, my sister, is nigh to hear your praise.
                                        [*A pause.*
And now, when they come, with your welcome the
   heavens rend!
            [*The crowd disperses, and* POLLUX *remains
                  alone in front of the stage.*

SCENE II

POLLUX, ELECTRA.

ELECTRA.
Prince, I must flee, now Helen is returning.
With every hour that goes my torments climb.
The fits of my fury have seized me again in the
   night-time,
And I tremble, and am bewildered, and all my soul
   is burning.

POLLUX.
Helen herself shall soothe your soul to peace.
She hates you not! And both of you shall forget
Ills suffered, and all passing grief and fret,
And murders covered long by the sweet soil of
      Greece.

ELECTRA.
Never! I bear too proud a soul to fear
Memories that grow more bitter year by year.

HELEN OF SPARTA

POLLUX.
O child, let the future sleep! Foolish it is to be
    fretting!
The days pass, and the grief grows distant, and the
    brain remembers no more . . .
Your forehead is too pure to be ever clouded o'er.
Only the gods have the right of never forgetting.

ELECTRA.
Hate I must, and hate I will.
My eyes have been taught to see nothing but crime
    on crime,
Draped in the purple of kings, rolled down the
    steeps of time.
My arms, and my hands, and my fingers have
    touched no thing save death;
And my eyes have seen nothing but Fate in fury
    pursuing still
The race of Atrides and dogging my father with
    panting breath;
And bloody hands I behold steeped in the blood of
    my mother,
And, fleeing the light of day, a murderer who is my
    brother
With all the guilt of my blood-stained race on his
    frenzied head.

POLLUX.
You were a child when the war burst into flame.
Helen with Paris her lover to Troy had fled,
Suspecting not that her flight would awaken the
    world to succour her shame.
Happy now she returns, and she and her spouse shall
    be met
With a welcome sweet in the town that I am the
    lord of yet.

HELEN OF SPARTA

ELECTRA.

I have seen Sparta to-day astir in the young dawn's
    red,
And the wakemen signalling from all the towers,
And blossomed boughs waving in the hard and
    virgin air,
And arches risen made of flame and flowers—
And I felt in the depth of my spirit death settle and
    make his lair.

POLLUX.

Let me call back to your mind—and the great gods
    know it is true—
How with a burning zeal I ever defended you
Against your own mad raging in your desperate days.
Hardly you felt the puissance of my healing
Over your forehead like a summer shadow stealing.
And some day, if the King had not returned,
Your name and mine with blended glory might
    have burned;
All this country, Argos and Sparta, might have been
    yours and mine,
And we should have ruled over our peoples in peace;
But Menelaus returns, and the sceptre I must resign,
And my fate frowns, and bids my dreaming cease.

ELECTRA.

And yet you know that Helen it is who has lit
This fire in my heart that I feed with my vengeful
    dreams.
This passion that parches me, she is the cause of it.
She it is whom I fear, fear like a fire that streams
In the dead of the night around me, with flaring
    and leaping sheaves.
If Menelaus had never wended his way to her,
My heart would have rested ever, like a nest in leaves
Hidden away in quiet that storms do not stir.

And I should be listening still to my mother and
    my sire
Speaking gently at evening, near the fire.
Their black blood the soil of Sparta would not cover,
Aegisthus had not been my mother's lover,
And the dread thing that floats before my eyes had
    never tortured me,
This vision of gashed limbs livid and streaming;
And I should not fear to go wherever it may be,
Haggard, tormented, fatal, mad
As Orestes in alien lands rending himself and
    screaming.

POLLUX.
How far, O child, are peace and calm from your
    mind,
When a sage counsel stings you as with pain.

ELECTRA.
What boots sage counsel to a frenzied brain. . . .

POLLUX. [*Seeing the messenger enter.*]
Helen and Menelaus will be kind.
Tell them your secrets, fears, your every ill:
First see them, and flee after, if you will.

SCENE III

A Messenger, the People, POLLUX.

THE MESSENGER.
My lord, your brother Castor, returned from afar,
Craves converse with yourself alone.
                              [*Exit* ELECTRA.

HELEN OF SPARTA

POLLUX. [*Uneasy.*]
Tidings of ill hap? . . . Tell me what they are . . .

THE MESSENGER.
My lord, I know not.

POLLUX.   Go, I await him here.
                              [*Exit messenger.*
What dark and fatal thing will he make known?
What sudden outrage brings this man I fear
More than Orestes?   [*He ponders, apart.*

SIMONIDES. [*Amid the crowd, at the back of the stage.*]
Turn all of you, behold!
Here is the car of purple and gold
Crossing the plains,
With Menelaus holding the reins!
Look at the chargers blacker that jet,
And the crowds that are running and following yet,
With branished boughs and lifted hands
Waving welcome, in the heart of her own lands,
To Helen, Helen home again!

EUPHORAS.
You would think them gods, they are so tall and fair.

A MAN AMONG THE PEOPLE.
We shall see them better on the bridge down there.
                    [*The crowd stream out at the back of the
                                        stage.*

HELEN OF SPARTA

SCENE IV

CASTOR *and* POLLUX

CASTOR.
I return from a journey through lands that are loud
    with delight,
And what have I seen save our sister's loveliness?
I return dazzled, and with a heart raging by day
    and night,
Feverishly longing to hold what other arms possess.

POLLUX.
Did the King in his overweening pride make bold
    to slight
The sovereign power that these my hands yet hold?

CASTOR.
Oh! to have seen her thus in the full light's glory,
With all the sun on her shoulders of gold,
Helen the pride of Greece, Helen renowned in story,
And to think that these eyes, and these arms, and
    these hands,
And this radiant brow whereon majesty rests,
And this body darting aloft its fire-tipped breasts,
Should fall, like a thing washed up from the sea,
To this King with the blanched hair and the eyes
    grown dim.

POLLUX.
So, too, it seems to me;
But as the booty of war and as a slave
Helen was given to the King and belongs to him.

HELEN OF SPARTA

CASTOR.

Oh that I too had been with the war-frenzied crowd,
Who plunged into Troy when its wives at their
hearths wailed loud;
When into red pools of blood its great walls crashed,
Splitting their blocks over warriors bruised and
gashed!
When death roaring in flames made everything
bright!
I would have snatched Helen away from her falling
palace and her fright,
And over black pathways in the forest hid
I would have carried my booty through the night
As Aeneas with Creusa and Anchises did.

POLLUX.

Certes, the kindly gods would have led you aright.

CASTOR.

Oh how regret in my spirit stirs and stings
That I did not go with the Greeks in the great
days of fate!
What had I recked of vengeance and hate,
And hunger and thirst, and all that danger brings,
If I had been fleeing with Helen from sea to sea!
We should have lived alone, under a foreign sky,
Far from our native land, far from cities and men,
Drunken both with the mad wine of a love that
could never die.

POLLUX.

Alas, the heavens and the earth and the furies then
Would have dogged your steps and heaped on you
torments dire!
Zeus, her father, is yours as well, and your mind is
distraught
If you hold the bond that binds you to her as naught.

HELEN OF SPARTA

CASTOR.
No, no, I am mortal, Tyndareus is my sire.
The love in my heart in no wise injures the gods. My
    love is my fate.
What does it matter who I am, and who we are,
And that some day I shall reign in the heavens as a
    star?
I would not be God save to be more of a man,
And to love or hate with a greater love or hate.
Helen is not my sister, but in my eyes
The woman the scent of whose beauty o'er Europe
    and Asia ran,
Who governed cities blazing to the skies,
And the black storms that lash the seas along,
She whom I love with passion-throes that rise
So suddenly frenzied and red and strong
That I exult to feel the ravaging flame
Burn to the very marrow of my frame.
Ah! you do not know, you cannot understand
My heart's leaping, only to see her go past,
Only to see her hands to mine descending,
And to my upturned face her slow eyes bending,
And on my mouth, her breath, hot and fast.
No, you do not understand, nor ever can . . .

POLLUX.
I know that Helen is fair and Menelaus fierce and
    brave,
And that she is henceforth his chattel, and his slave.

CASTOR.
She belongs to the world ere she belongs to one man:
Her glory and her beauty are the terrible stakes,
On the earth that throbs, under the sky that shakes,
Of the battles of kings and men fighting wherever
    she is.

HELEN OF SPARTA

She belongs to him who abducts her and has her to
  love,
She is his most of all who guards her and keeps her
  his,
Even against the rape of the gods above,
Whose lust is ever lying in wait to spring.
Feeble and age-beridden is the King.

POLLUX.
He lives.

CASTOR.
    Nay, he trails heavily his limbs, and hoary eld
Sits mournfully upon his pallid brow.
His wavering eyes death have beheld.
His steps are slow upon his pathways now.

POLLUX.
He lives, I say.

CASTOR.
Oh why did he not perish in that night
When dizzy carnage reeled, hunting for more to slay,
When Ilium burned . . .

POLLUX.   He lives, I tell you, yet.

CASTOR.
Ah! with a red design my spirit is beset!
What matters if an old man lives or dies. . . .

POLLUX.
The man who knows his strength heeds not though
  all men chide him,
And follows his path, under the vast haggard skies,
With his implacable will to guide him:
Your fortune is your own affair and you should not
  forget. . . .

HELEN OF SPARTA

CASTOR.
I know, I know, and in my heart I do not doubt
That what I fear to do is but my duty:
Who, if not I, will rescue Helen's beauty
From an old King whose kisses are burnt out?
And whose old arms hang round her like a chain
So that her closed thighs shiver at his touch?
This love is a pretence, most vile and vain;
It cries to the skies; it is an outrage such
Helen must feel it tarnish and defile
The fairness of her body, mouth and eyes.
Oh! there are nights of horror when the stars grow
    pale
To look upon these loathsome kisses that assail
The Queen, and calls disaster down upon their
    bed . . .

POLLUX.
Oh! you are mad! and know not what your lips
    have said.

CASTOR. [*Continuing without paying heed.*]
The punishment will not wait for justice; to-day
    it hides
But only to rise the deadlier when the hour betides.
I shall choose my pitiless pleasure when I like:
Nothing shall stay the hand I raise to strike.

HELEN OF SPARTA

Scene V

Pollux, *Citizens, Shepherds, Soldiers, Maidens,
Youths, Old People,* Electra, Helen, Menelaus.

Pollux. [*At the back of the stage, calling the crowd
    back round the palace—joyously to the maidens.*]
Come hither ye, and rain your roses down in showers
Upon this stairway; heap before the palace door
    your best,
Yea, to the very threshold, so that Helen may rest
Her beautiful eyes on the reaped glory of the flowers.
        [*The whole crowd pours across the back of
            the stage, and the maidens scatter roses.*

An Old Man. [*Leaning over the balustrade.*]
How heavy with age is Menelaus, slow and seared!
How wrinkled his face, how white his beard!

A Shepherd.
Old man, canst thou on Menelaus gaze,
With Helen to be seen?

A Young Man. [*To the shepherd.*]
My father, a vine-dresser, who knew her in Troy,
Wept when he spoke of her beauty serene.
And with the radiant sweet vision of joy
Of her who is here returned from Asia, he cheered
His humble life to the last hour he lived, and then
Died with her name on his lips.

A Noble.   Never was woman endeared,
As she is, to numberless hosts of men.

HELEN OF SPARTA

A YOUNG MAN.
Upon our knees we desire her presence, and speak
    her name!

ANOTHER.
To the call of her eyes, ever, armies of heroes came.
The hair that covers her head is a golden flame.

A SHEPHERD. [*Looking down the valley.*]
See, the black horses are stopping! Look at their
    bits flecked with foam!

A YOUNG WOMAN. [*Leaning over the balustrade.*]
The cloak she is wearing is the one
That Agamemnon gave her at Mycenae, long ago.

ANOTHER WOMAN. [*Pushing her children in front
    of her.*]
Let the little ones stand in the first row;
For some day their eyes must remember, when the
    long years have run,
How they rested on Helen coming home.
                [*The guards marshal the crowd in front of
                HELEN and MENELAUS, who, entering
                the stage by the monumental staircase,
                keep in the background.*]

POLLUX. [*To MENELAUS.*]
My Lord and King, this is the day that crowns my
    vows:
After a score of years of grief and war and butchery,
Victors at last of Troy and of the sea,
You both return in triumph to your royal house.
I am your servant from this hour:
My sovereignty I here resign,
And to the gods I pray they will make these hands
    of mine

HELEN OF SPARTA

Two loyal forces and staunch upholders of your
power.   [*The regalia are brought in.*
Here to your hands the sceptre and the fillet I
restore.

A NOBLE. [*To* MENELAUS, *pointing to* POLLUX.]
And I, King Menelaus, will tell you more:
In all these years neither your gardens nor your
palaces,
Nor the rich hives, gay with golden honey, of your
bees,
Nor the white flocks that browse your pastures o'er,
Nor yet your heavy cattle with their warm breath
scenting hay,
Have lacked his vigilance the time you were away.
Prone to no party, in counsel he was sage;
Ere obstacles he faced, their magnitude he would
gauge;
Quarrels he soothed, and would not suffer blood to
be spilt.
Five bridges cross the Eurotas, by him built,
And hamlets down the lower river reaches
Are joined with farms, and pasture-lands, and
beaches.
Righteously he has reigned, an incorruptible Prince.
But what imports all this, O Menelaus, since
To-day with Helen you return, victorious and serene.

A MAIDEN. [*Leaving a group and addressing* HELEN.]
Our mothers would say to us, round the hearth in
the evening hours,
Thinking of your loveliness that dazzles the day,
" Never your eyes will behold what gladdened ours,
For Helen is in Troy, and Asia is far away."
But now you are returned, O Queen,

HELEN OF SPARTA

The beauty our mothers remembered we ourselves
    have seen
Living, walking, smiling, shedding its rays
On Sparta, with its radiance lighting our ways.
And our vows are heard, and we may be sure
    that we,
Having seen you before us immaculately bright,
We shall speak of you to children yet to be,
As our mothers spoke to us by the fire at night.
               [She gives flowers to HELEN.

MENELAUS. [*In the centre of the stage.*]
Now I remember no more life and its ills and fears,
And the wild war, and all those who have died,
And the storm poised o'er vessels in their pride,
Since Helen is mine again, and Sparta's welcome
    rings in my ears.
I yield myself to the gods and in my subjects I
    confide.   [*To* POLLUX.
Pollux, whom Zeus chose to be King in my stead,
That day I gat me to the chances of the sea,
Now after twenty years my thanks to you be said,
For keeping this my realm of Sparta safe for me.
Your care has multiplied my thriving flocks;
To the watering-place I see my cattle going,
I see my sure-foot goats climbing the rocks;
And my forests and fields and meadows, as hither I
    came, were showing
Your skilful vigilance and attentive hand.
Thanks.—Firmly and wisely you have ruled my
    land,
In calm, profound and necessary peace.
                  [*To the crowd of citizens.*
And to you also, vinedressers, shepherds, and sowers,
    thanks,
All you whose fertile labours never cease,

HELEN OF SPARTA

At your firesides, and at the mountain's foot, and by
    the river's banks,
You who have heaped my realm with plenty, every-
    where.
And while the earth where we fought was red as a
    wound that bleeds,
While slaughter called us on to blacker deeds,
Only of plants and wool your busy hands had care,
And of the grapes of your vines, and the corn you
    had sown.
Each of you, toiling but for his own,
With firm and ready arms laboured for all our needs.
You have made this land, the sweetest boon of life,
More fertile, and Sparta fairer to behold.
With forethought you have killed the rankling strife
That like a herd of wolves harassed you of old.
And so I believe you happy, and know you are
    faithful and good,
And my heart is exalted now that I have returned,
Safe from tempests at last and the shedding of blood,
And henceforth I can rest me in ease well-earned,
In my festive country and house that is full of joy.
           [MENELAUS, *taking* HELEN's *hand, walks*
               round the stage. The crowd is ranged
               in a circle round the threshold of the
               palace.
                 At this moment, behind the crowd,
               but at the forefront of the stage, ELEC-
               TRA *appears. She drags her steps, as*
               though she came in spite of herself.

ELECTRA. [*To the* L. *of the stage, in the front rank.*]
O my eyes, you shall not look on her! Look away!
She is Death, home from Troy, prowling about for
    prey!
And if these others from the peril do not flee,

270

HELEN OF SPARTA

It is because none of them sees what you can see.
I will not, will not raise
My eyes to look at her! My eyes, you shall not
    gaze!
> [*As she speaks these words, slowly* ELECTRA'S
> *eyes turn towards* HELEN, *who ap-*
> *proaches and passes, without noticing*
> *her.*

Oh what a stately grace her loveliness hath!
How tranquil the fall of her feet on the rose-strewn
    path!
O power! O beauty! how fateful art thou to see,
And how despite myself I feel thee entering me,
Curbing my heart to thy fell sovereignty,
But not to shine therein, to rend it utterly!
> [HELEN *has reached the threshold of the*
> *palace. At the moment she ascends the*
> *steps,* ELECTRA, *as though maddened:*

Helen! Helen! Helen!
> [*The crowd, repeating* ELECTRA'S *words,*
> *but with the tones of exaltation.*
> Helen! Helen! Helen!
> [ELECTRA'S *anguish is absorbed, as it were,*
> *by the general enthusiasm.*
> HELEN *and* MENELAUS *turn round,*
> *and enter the palace.*]

CURTAIN

271

ACT II

Scene I

Helen *and* Menelaus

Helen. [*To* Menelaus.]
SO then, I have slumbered calmly and peacefully
In my own home, the first time for twenty
years,
Facing the night's on-coming without a heart full
of fears,
Keeping my sad body for you alone and for me.
I have not asked if it has kept its charms
To tempt your eyes, to lure your hands and arms;
And my heart, in its new fidelity blest,
Has enjoyed the ample sweetness of being tired and
at rest.
I am yours ever, and I thank you for having passed
The sea to rescue me from shame,
And for having snatched my beauty from that Asian
town at last,
To clothe it again in the glory of a dear and royal
name.

Menelaus.
Nay, all this country of Greece was resolute to save
Helen my spouse, and her cause, too great for me,
was a whole land's;
From the mountain summits to the heart of the
plains and the far sea-sands,

HELEN OF SPARTA

As with one leap, magnificently brave,
A people rushed, with your name on their passionate
    lips.
You were the splendour they worshipped, erect at
    the sky-line;
And, rising on waves the tempests buffeted, ships
Lifted their prows to you and plunged through the
    brine.

HELEN.

Friend, let that fatal glory perish! When I recall
The pangs it has cost me, my heart yet shudders in
    stark affright;
My beauty is dying, alas! under a heavy pall
As the day dies, shrouded in the silent night.
If my eyes still open and seek the light,
Let it be you they see, my native heavens that
    gladdened me when
My beauty was yet unconscious of the curse.
Oh! crystal air, in the sun quivering, how I will
    immerse
My body in your deeps of calm to make me pure
    again!

MENELAUS.

You shall gather into your brain the sweetness of
    days gone by,
In dawns serene and evenings full of quiet grace,
Near fountains in whose waters our forests sigh.

HELEN.

When the wind blew from Argolis and Thrace
To Troy, I dreamed of this by the sea-shore.
Of a sudden I saw the terrace and the white palace
    door,

HELEN OF SPARTA

And the portico, and the massed flowers of the
    garden where
You welcomed me first with a bridegroom's hot
    embrace.
And I could hear the dog barking there,
And the steps of the shepherd on the mossy flags,
And the familiar song of Lydian slave-girls driving
To the warm stable the herd that lags.
Thus at evening I would listen to all these memories
    reviving,
And prowling like a thief that would not be seen;
And my heart found itself again and remembered
    you.

MENELAUS.
A stranger and a Trojan woman you have never
    been.

HELEN. [*Drawing* MENELAUS *to a rose-tree, then to
    the statue of a faun.*]
See, this is the rose I planted with my own hands
The day Agamemnon had built Mycenæ anew;
Rose-tree of pride, in the day's full glare it stands,
But its leaves are gentle, and its roses are flowers of
    peace.
And the ivy there knows me again, I am sure, for I
Twisted it like a flexible sheaf, and made it lie
At the feet of this big, old faun, with his head's
    shagged fleece:
The faun is o'er-run by the numberless foliage now,
And I can see nothing of him but his flute and his
    brow.

MENELAUS.
Everything recollects you, and happy nature tries
In its echoes to bring back to life your ringing cries

HELEN OF SPARTA

When you wrestled, valiant and naked, by the river
   reeds
With those who tamed my stormy steeds.

HELEN.

Oh! since then what pain has been mine in passion's
   maze,
And how far, alas, are those olden games with their
   stalwart pride!
Now I will ask but for the tranquil days
Of a wife who guards and tends her own fireside
With hands, fain to serve, that are gentle and do
   not tire:
I who have known such furious flames flaring to
   burn down my will,
Now I adore the lamp and love the household fire.
And you and I will live alone, loving each other a
   little still,
Accepting without flinching our existence gray,
And the weight of the numerous years, heavier from
   day to day.

MENELAUS.

For me you will always be the passionate Queen
Whose forehead is firm and rosy and by nothing
   tarnished yet.

HELEN.

Oh the body's decline! Stinging regret!
The setting of too many suns these eyes have seen!
But to-day I return to you with a chastened soul,
And my heart knows what certain happiness it lost
   by fleeing
From your calm house and tender love's control.
And I bring to you my different being,
And a woman strangely changed to live with you.

275

HELEN OF SPARTA

MENELAUS.
The gods are ever attentive to such vows!

HELEN.
Of old, when I came to you a faithful spouse,
To your tranquil love, the first love ever I knew,
With a heart that was faithful to you and rich in
    your love of it,
You said—on this very bench where now I sit—
              [*Sitting down on a bench to the* L.
" The grapes of my vine are grapes of fire,
My herds are heavy, my cellars wide;
I do not feel in my heart the mad desire
Of rushing at Death and snatching victory from his
    side.
My love will burn but with a radiance pure,
Which shall aye watch o'er your youth and over
    your fate;
But my tenderness at least shall be tenacious and
    sure,
And if you but love me a little, my love for you
    shall be great."
Not without a murmur did I listen to you then,
But now I can remember the very sound of your
    voice.

MENELAUS.
My love endureth ever and shall not cease;
What I said in that hour more than ever I swear it
    again,
And my soul is enchanted, and proudly I rejoice. . . .

HELEN.
What your heart tells me fills my heart with peace.
Your heart is noble, tranquil, and sure, and loves
    me so

H E L E N   O F   S P A R T A

That to hear its converse my just remorse sinks low.
But from myself I will save myself to-day,
And from the fear and the danger of having a frame
    of flesh.—
The urgent hour now calls for you to go—
See, at the threshold of the house the shadow wanes.

MENELAUS.
As Queen and mistress you shall govern it afresh,
Sagely fulfilling what its simple fate ordains.

HELEN.
Before the western rim pillows the sun,
The serving women's tasks will all be done.
But you to the Council now must hie,
Where all, even Castor, will be guided by your will.
Farewell. I know what tasks I have to fill,
And I shall see you again when the hours that race
Bring back the white flocks to the watering-place.
        [MENELAUS *directs his steps to the assembly,*
           which is held behind the palace.

SCENE II

CASTOR *and* HELEN

Enter CASTOR. *Accompanied by citizens, he is on his
    way to the assembly. Suddenly, seeing* HELEN,
    who is on the point of entering the Palace, he
    stops short. He leaves the group of Nobles and
    approaches her, impulsively.*

CASTOR. [*To those accompanying him.*]
Go. I will join you in the Council by and by.
                [*To* HELEN.
Helen, listen to what my violent heart now saith.

277

HELEN OF SPARTA

Your name in my maddened soul sings wild and
   loud,
And my blood is dark with tempests driving to death.
Yesterday when I saw you again and when all the
   crowd
Stretched out their arms to you, like a forest bending
   in the storm,
Fain had I mastered and forced back their surging
   tide,
And carried you off, alone with you, I know not
   where, to hide.
All the night in the dark and in my dreams I have
   seen your form;
My hot, quick breath burned on your rosy brow;
I bruised you in my fury which, alas, was ended
   soon,
For the vision faded with the paling of the moon.

HELEN.
You! You! O ye gods! Castor, my own brother,
   now!

CASTOR.
I want you, Helen, with a sudden violence!
I am not one to tarry on the brink.
I am not one to feign and make pretence,
And say what in his jealous heart he does not think;
I love with rage; with bitterness I hate;
And now I go, crying to your terrified heart that I
   will make you,
Ere many days have run, free to follow my fate!

HELEN.
Never!

CASTOR. [*As he leaves the stage.*]
     I want you, Helen, and I will take you.

HELEN OF SPARTA

Scene III

Helen *and* Electra

HELEN.
O this shame once again covering my destiny,
Like a muddy foam crawling over the sea!
O ye gods! Into what perils are you dragging me
    yet,
And by what passions still is my body beset!
I had come home to the Atrides' land to end my life
In peace, pressing my mantle's folds around my
    breast . . .
Oh these torrid desires that flame around me and
    grant me no rest . . .
Oh these confessions of passion that stab like a knife!
    [*To* Electra, *who approaches her.*
Tell me, you, whose hate I have earned and of
    which I am sure,
You whose father died cursing Helen who brought
    his consort to shame,
You whose brother with cries of horror utters my
    name,
Heap my heart with the words that are hardest to
    endure.

ELECTRA.
I cannot hate you when I look into your eyes,
And when I come close to you my rancour dies.

HELEN.
These haggard hands of mine have wasted your days
    on earth,
Robbed you of candour and faith and joy and mirth.

HELEN OF SPARTA

I am she who is ever attended by crime,
Outrage precipitous, treason that bides its time.
I am the night that covers you, the ruin you welter
in,
I am the sorrow that prowls about your house and
kin;
And I reign, and am unpunished, and am a well-
loved wife.
I it was who sharpened Clytemnestra's knife;
But for me, Agamemnon would still be Mycenæ's
king;
Orestes over the face of the earth would not be
wandering.
I alone am your death.

ELECTRA.　　　　　You alone are my life.
I remember no longer all that was of yore;
Vengeance, pride, envy I know no more.
I love you, and love to tell you of my love.

HELEN. [*Aghast.*]
You also! You!

ELECTRA.　　　All my being yearns for you!
To your voice I listen with rapture that never I
knew,
Even when it chides me, and haply bids me depart!

HELEN.
Go away! Go away!

ELECTRA.　　　　　O sweet and bitter smart!
But to hear Helen's voice
My heart is full of the tempest of this joy and pain!
Oh! the breeze that is blowing now, the plain,

HELEN OF SPARTA

The mountains and the forests are full of our love
 and rejoice.
Oh this fever of fear and savage ecstacy!

HELEN.
Go away! I will not hearken to your mad imaginings!
Heaven shudders with horror hearing what you say
 to me!

ELECTRA.
No, no! Heaven hears not lovers' quarrellings!
For heaven's own flames are hearts, and its great
 winds are wings
Which as they sweep through the air mingle in
 rapture's mesh;
The flowers with their calyces bared wide are kisses
 made flesh;
All the waves, that the storm on the ocean's face
Shakes in a cruel spasm, swell and enlace:
Nay, in the vastness of the skies above,
There are stars of gold that love as the gods love.

HELEN.
O the horror of home-coming!

ELECTRA.   Listen!
You are lovely ever, and you shall not drive me
 away.
Yesterday I hated you; I am yours to-day.
You are the only fire of gold that in my night will
 glisten;
You are the sudden sunshine in the black sky,
She who with gracious ears hearkens a sad heart's
 praying,
She who has suffered too much to deny.

H.ELEN OF SPARTA

HELEN.
Unhappy woman!

ELECTRA.　　　I feel that my fate to yours is wed.
Alas! for how many days have I been straying,
Sombre and solitary, morose and harsh, with no-
　　where to hide my head!
And with what a weight of memories that heavier
　　grow
Must I drag this broken body, whither I do not
　　know.
With eyes grown great by gazing on anguish and
　　fear
I have suffered in Mycenæ, Tirynthus, and here,
And what could I love under the vast golden sky
But vengeance, and hate of the gods till I die!

HELEN.
Poor pitiful soul, deceived wherever it turns,
As Helen's is, why wert thou ever born?

ELECTRA.
My fate it is to feel in my heart forlorn
Only a fire I fear that bites and burns.
Oh this hurtling step of the Furies of the night
Which rings within my pale and bruisèd flesh,
And treads me down, and drags me onward, and
　　maddens me ever afresh!
And lo! now I feel love in my breast, raging and
　　roaring,
And I weep and cry out and perish while my heart
　　is imploring.

HELEN.
Cast out of your spirit utterly, for you must,
Like a pack of ravenous wolves leaping around their
　　prey,
282

HELEN OF SPARTA

Like the plague and death, cast out these mad desires
    of lust,
Which are an outrage far too foul for lips to say.

ELECTRA.
No, no! I cannot! My frenzy is too fleet,
And farther than my reason peers it springs.
I drink with bliss the subtle poison sweet
Which goads my sad flesh with its aching stings.
I am Atreus' daughter: death's shadow is round my
    head.
Ere I came to you to utter my mad imaginings,
I had spurned my shame and denied my dead;
I have not listened to what they were saying under
    the sod;
When the love of you entered into me, on their
    lonely ashes I trod,
And on their pride, and my vengeance for which I
    should live;
And lo! here of a sudden madly your heart I assail!
Take me and tame me, pity me and forgive!
Electra who was austere abandons her heart and is
    frail.

HELEN.
Never! As long as the gods are masters of my fate,
Your fingers shall not touch my body!
        [ELECTRA *leaves* HELEN *and, overpowered
        by pain, sinks down on the bench where
        * MENELAUS *and* HELEN *had sat. She
        does not see* POLLUX *entering, and
        * POLLUX *does not see her.*

HELEN OF SPARTA

Scene IV

Pollux, Electra, Helen

POLLUX. [*To* HELEN.]   Sister, I know
With what a flame, frightful and reprobate,
My brother burns for your beauty, and haply he has
   confessed,
Scorning both my anger and your glory,
The frantic fury in his wretched breast.

ELECTRA. [*Darting up from the bench.*]
Oh! fire more monstrous than my fatal story!
                                        [*To* HELEN.
Was it for this that you hurled back my outstretched
   hand?
Are crime and incest what your lusts demand,
And the shocks of the brute loves that bruise the
   flesh?

POLLUX.
Electra!

HELEN. [*To* POLLUX.]
                  Listen to her, listen to her, I say to you!
She at last o'erwhelms me with the words that are
   my due.

ELECTRA.
You arms of men, vices of pride and dizzy desire
That cruelly crush our bodies virgin and fresh;
You vows of men, brasiers of crime and madness;
   wild
Arms that seize us in lust; panting breath on fire;
Spasms that gush forth from our flesh torn and
   defiled

HELEN OF SPARTA

Under a fiery tempest of kisses and teeth;
And you, hands of men whose prey we are, beneath
War's crumbling walls when the reeking blood
    pours horrible to see;
You who made Troy town flare to the skies
Only to see the havoc glassed in our staring eyes;
I hate you, I hate you, for taking Helen from me,
And her mighty love and her burning tenderness,
And for having worn with grief and pain the heart
That I love ever, although it bids me depart.
                              [*Exit, furiously.*

HELEN.
Do you conceive, O Pollux, my fear and my distress,
And under what a burden I must cross my threshold
    presently,
O you, the oldest of my kin, whose counsels true
Strengthened of old my reason as it grew.
Eyes fixed on me of a sudden covet me;
Lips that come near to mine of a sudden seethe;
The hand held out to mine is moist and fain would
    cleave;
And you would say that the wind's lips breathe
A hunger for my throat when they touch it at eve.
When the crowd follows my steps and around me
    treads,
I dare not utter a blessing on their heads
For fear a dumb desire should rise on the air.

POLLUX.
Let not your soul, unhappy sister, yield to despair.

HELEN.
To say that I hoped to live my life in peace,
When here I returned, whither my heart had pre-
    ceded me,

HELEN OF SPARTA

To my native land, my fair sweet land of Greece,
To the land that sheltered my pure, calm infancy!
Your rivers and forests, O Greece, your sun and
  your shade,
Did they not promise their help and all their might,
If ever my outworn heart were again afraid?
When your shores dawned on the sea's rim my soul
  sang out in delight;
And my feet and my hands and my whole body
  thrilled
At the touch of your soil with the living sources
  filled
Of sinuous rivers and cataracts hurled from the
  height.
I have been at home for a day, and the stones ruined
  lie
Of the fronton of gold my dream built on high.
And oh to be back in Troy with its red hecatomb
Of warriors locked in the death-grip in the night's
  gloom!
Who shall restore my wandering life, from ocean to
  ocean blown,
And the couch honied with bewildering scent
On which my guilty body lay indifferent
With never a cry of passion, but at least without a
  moan
Of horror, for it is here, in my native land, among
  my own,
That a virgin and a brother have taught me indeed
To what rash heights of crime a monstrous love can
  rise.

POLLUX.
I see, my sister, how horror and surprise
Have bitten into your soul and made it bleed.
But if you crave my counsel in your doubt,

H E L E N   O F   S P A R T A

Fear not, by night or day, to seek me out.
But why is not Menelaus ready to help you with
    his sovran powers?

HELEN.

O let him know nothing, not even this talk of ours:
He is getting old; he has suffered; his strength is
    failing;
When his vessel near the Dorian land was sailing,
And when his tearful eyes gazed on the hills of
    Greece,
I swore that never again he should weep for my
    sake.
Henceforth my tender love shall over him wake,
And nothing of me he shall know, that his life may
    have peace.
To you it is that Helen comes in her distress,
You who do love me with a brother's tenderness.

POLLUX.

Of a truth, I have my plans: I know which road
    to tread
To the fixed goal where the crown of my destiny
    lies;
Nevertheless, do not believe that my soul is dead;
I cannot in silence look into your eyes;
But my strong determination cheerfully stills
My heart's stirrings, when my ambition wills.

HELEN.

I trust in you; besides, in whom else could I trust?
On whom could I count if you should not be sure,
If the words I hear you speak were but a trap and a
    lure?
I will live far from you, and trouble you not unless
    I must,

HELEN OF SPARTA

Knowing your arm safeguards my loneliness;
I have too much pride ever to be moaning my distress;
And you will never know how sad I am and tired
By twenty years of passion I have not desired.

Scene V

Nobles, Pollux, Helen, Menelaus, Castor

At this moment a crowd, surrounding Menelaus *and speaking to him, hurry tumultuously across the stage. They come from the assembly hall.*

A Noble. [*To* Menelaus.]
Sire, I am sure that Castor no wise knew
How cruel were the words he spoke to you.

Another.
He seemed to be lost to himself, and in the grips
Of a mad rage that stifled his cries as they rose to
his lips.

Another.
Those who feel that their cause is his, were stirred
By shame to hear him raving!

Pollux. [*To the Noble.*]
Tell me, what has occurred?

The Noble. [*To* Pollux.]
Castor in the assembly has insulted the King
With harsh, quick cries of venomous sting . . .

288

HELEN OF SPARTA

MENELAUS.
My soul that recks not all its calmness keeps;
And I will not have you desolate these happy days
Because of a sudden the madness is ablaze
That Castor like a brazier hid in his bad heart's
    deeps.

POLLUX.
O sire, your justice by your goodness is exceeded;
But Castor is guilty, and the days are no more
When for his temper and his headstrong whims I
    pleaded.

MENELAUS.
He is your brother, and Helen's too.

POLLUX.
Certes, Leda bore all three of us, and the one who
Died by a red death at Mycenæ of yore;
But only Helen and I under the wing were con-
    ceived
Of the pure and dazzling swan that the clouds of
    Olympus cleaved
And to earth descended to pierce my mother with
    his amorous fire.
He it was whose spirit fills me with the pride and
    the desire
Of being sincere in zeal and soul alway.
He it was who helped me to reign, as he helps me
    to obey.

CASTOR. [*Entering in his turn. Surrounded by several
    partisans, he crosses the back of the stage.*]
Do not listen to them, Helen: their mouths have
    ever lied.

HELEN OF SPARTA

I alone do what I say.
I am only a tamer of horses by the river reaches,
But my heart is too proud for flattering speeches.

POLLUX.
Castor! Castor!

CASTOR. I leave that care to you, my brother bold,
You who are lavish of words and honied talk;
But I will denounce your skill in deceit; and your
    plans I will baulk
Of turning the favouring hour to profit when kings
    are old.
> [*His adherents drag him violently from the
> stage.*

CURTAIN

ACT III

Scene I

Electra, Menelaus, Pollux

ELECTRA.

AND now you know, as I do, what a host
Of parching memories my spirit blight,
Conceive the terror that haunts me day and night,
Visited as I am by ghost on ghost.

MENELAUS.
I have long known, nay, I ever knew
That murder is nigh, alas, when an Atrides strides
On the black, torrid pathway of his loves. But you,
Child, you are like the sunshine that divides
Tempests dashed on the sea from swollen skies.
The blood you have seen poured out like rain
Has sullied not the mirror of your limpid eyes.
You were young then; and in your dreaming brain
You understood not these mad murders reddening
        the night,
Crimes that with crimson horror terrified the light.
Your heart was innocent of all . . .

ELECTRA.   Alas! It understood;
It knows that ravaging passion drives along
Like a black plague, and that nothing is so strong
Under the skies kindled with the flame of bad men's
        blood,

HELEN OF SPARTA

As the song of the life of love or its death's cry.
And it knows as well that destiny plays
At mocking kings in these disastrous days,
And that the words on human lips do nothing but
  lie,
And that Castor hates you, and fain would rid
Your Sparta of its chief and Helen of her spouse.
Oh violent secrets in my heart are hid!

MENELAUS.
Castor's desires grope blindly, and cannot reach this
  brow's
Calm majesty whence peacefully I rule this land;
I have lived too long close to peril to be timorous of
  the hand
Of one who in my own house, for a child's whim,
Lets the wild roll of anger master him.
For see you, I have never, all my life long,
Tasted such happiness as in these hours how deep
Which have brought back to me the love secure
Of her who from the world's end came to me.
You will never know, my child, how she can soothe
  to sleep
Unfertile cares in hearts wont to endure;
No, nor how sweet my life and death shall be,
Tended by her tranquil hands, in the light of her
  loving eyes.

ELECTRA.
And yet, if this happiness you dream of . . .

MENELAUS. [*Indulgently.*]   Say no more!
Besides, Pollux is not the man they can surprise.
He watches his brother, and serves his King zealously.
Did you not see how fervently he upbore
My sovran power outraged by Castor?

HELEN OF SPARTA

He can reign or obey, according as fate decrees.
It may be that some day, if so I please,
After my death, in this Palace he will be master . . .
He will know how to command, since he knows
    how to obey,
For his soul is loyal, and his heart as clear as day.
You see, then, waking or sleeping, I am safe, out of
    harm's reach,
In the peace of long days, and of hours alike, each
    to each.

ELECTRA.
Castor is wholly violent, his madness seethes . . .
Send him away from Sparta, far from where Helen
    breathes.

MENELAUS.
Pollux will hold him, if he is my foe.

ELECTRA.
O heart too kind, still resolute to know
Nothing of hate! O confidence insensate, blind . . .

MENELAUS. [*Smiling.*]
My child . . . Lo, now the evening falls, with
    shadows soft,
And into the stifling day comes the sea-wind;
Come, let us climb the dark hill from whose summit
    oft
I have shown you, in the days long distant, where
The roads to Argos and Tirynthus part.
There you shall tell me again the tale of the grief
    in your heart,
And I will smile, listening to your grim despair.
                [*To* POLLUX, *who enters.*
Pollux, will you not come with us into the woods?

HELEN OF SPARTA

POLLUX.
I have come to say to the shepherds that to-morrow
    with the sun
They must take the flocks to the marshes where
    shallow rivers run,
And shear the ewes, and dry the fleeces while the
    day is hot,
And pen the bucks in separate folds, ere the day is
    done.

MENELAUS.
Farewell!

> [*Exit with* ELECTRA *by the path which
> leads to the mountain.*

SCENE II

POLLUX *and* CASTOR

POLLUX.
I was seeking you.

CASTOR.   That you had found me not!
It was not to you my steps were guiding me.

POLLUX.
I know that my advice is to your wrath a sting,
And that in me you hate the man who serves the
    King.

CASTOR.
I hate you all. But Menelaus, he
Unpunished guards and keeps, under his roof, in his
    bed,
Her whose beauty makes my soul a haggard thing.
I can wait no longer; all ablaze is my head;

HELEN OF SPARTA

And I feel myself carried away by my fever, fiercely
    burning,
By the leaps of my heart, by the cries of my yearn-
    ing,
As by a storm whose fury never tires.
I am haunted. Everywhere I see Helen's face . . .
My dreams devour her flesh with their greedy fires;
Her naked flanks I storm with my desires . . .
And Menelaus mocks me, he has stolen my place.
I have my plans. I know he is yonder. I am going.

POLLUX. [*Scoffing.*]
I did not even need to show him the way.

SCENE III

POLLUX, *the Shepherds*, HELEN, *the Crowd*

POLLUX. [*To the chief of the shepherds, who enters.
The others follow.*]
Shepherd, to-morrow with the dawn of day,
Lead to the marshlands where the sweet streams are
    flowing,
And where the dense new grass is good to browse,
All the herd of sheep and cows,
With the folded lambs, and the goats that love to
    roam.
And now, to turn to another matter,
Tell me the village chatter,
Concerning Menelaus and his coming home.

THE CHIEF SHEPHERD.
Sparta had eyes only for Helen's eyes.
Some I know who have kissed the vain dust that lies
Where her feet fell.

HELEN OF SPARTA

The King is old; he has one foot in the grave;
He has brought his fame from Asia with him over
    the wave;
But you are regretted, and waited for again,
'Though silent are the mouths of men.
      [*A pause.*—Pollux *seems to be listening.*—
         The shepherd is about to withdraw.
Forgive me, haply I had too much to tell.

Pollux.
No, no, it is my pleasure to linger in this spot.
Tell me, I fain would know your lot,
      [*He listens and speaks absent-mindedly.*
And whether happiness dowers you with peace,
And if your household tend
Your flocks and farm, and by their toil increase
Your wealth from year's end to year's end?
                  [*He listens.*
Tell me, you see what man before you stands,
Placing his hand on your shoulder, and taking it
    away,
Stepping aside from you, seizing your staff in his
    hands
And bending it? And you hear what he has to say?
Shepherd, look at me well; hearken to Pollux, who
To the land's ancient customs ever is true;
Pollux who asks how you fare, and nothing disdains
Which to the welfare of his shepherds appertains.

The Chief Shepherd.
My lord, such gracious words . . .

Pollux. [*Interrupting him, somewhat feverishly.*]
Times are hard, life is full of toil,
And the incessant care given to the herds
Does not for ever foil

The tortuous perfidy of disease.
What man is there can count on certain ease
After his labour, and sustenance all the year?

THE CHIEF SHEPHERD.
My lord, when you were King, we were persuaded
That your fertile spirit, supple and clear,
Freed our walls from danger and fear;
We were wont to say: "By the gracious gods he is
    aided."
            [*A shepherd has just appeared, descending
            the mountain path in the background.
            POLLUX has risen, and looks anxiously
            at the shepherd.*

THE SHEPHERD. [*As he sees* POLLUX.]
The King has been slain, up in the mountain there!
            [*Consternation. The shepherd is surrounded
            and questioned.*

POLLUX.
By whom?

A SHEPHERD.
        What 's this?

THE SHEPHERD. [*Who has come down from the
    mountain.*]   By Castor!

THE CROWD.   O Menelaus!

A SHEPHERD.   The King!
        [*Tumult.—Enter* HELEN *from the Palace,
        leaning, in great distress and half
        fainting, on the peristyle.*

HELEN OF SPARTA

HELEN.
What? . . . Where? . . .
These crowds, these cries, these shouts . . . the
    King!
Say what you know . . . Brother, what have they
    said?

POLLUX.
Alas! my sister, fate is hostile and would dismay us!
Oh what a terrible sorrow on Hellas is shed!

HELEN.
Dead?

POLLUX. Castor, our brother, has slain Menelaus.

HELEN.
Ye gods! Ye gods!

POLLUX.   Oh bloody and terrible surprise!
Struck in the hearts of both of us, broken now are
    the ties
Which bound our souls to this man sick and
    demented.
I will relent no more than he relented;
I will show forth the crime, how black it is and red,
Nor heed within my bosom nature's cries.

HELEN.
Lead me yonder where Menelaus lies dead!

THE SHEPHERD.
When I came running they were bringing him back
Where through the vineyards runs the mountain
    track.
You will find him in the Palace now, on his bed.
They had closed his eyes; calm was his white face.

HELEN OF SPARTA

HELEN.
O King, that I had loved you more! Woe on my
race!
[HELEN, *overcome, is supported into the Palace.*

POLLUX. [*To the shepherd.*]
Electra was with Menelaus. What did she do?

THE SHEPHERD.
I saw her staunching the wound as it streamed.
A staring light in her mad eyes gleamed:
Round the body on her knees she crept,
And her moans clomb to an agony. Then up she
leapt,
And rushed to where the mighty forest looms,
To look for Castor in its maze of glooms.

POLLUX.
Now from the walls let flowers and branches vanish;
With copious tears our noble dead be wept,
While horror-stricken Sparta brands this crime
Of a blind murderer whom I banish.
[*The crowd swells, nobles, husbandmen,
women, children, but noiselessly.*
The assassin's hand, O King, denies thee time
To taste the fruits with which my loyal industry
Has laden in thy country every tree.
Just thou wert, and calm, and wise, and thy good
name
Was of a purer ray than Agamemnon's golden fame.
Unsullied was the sceptre in thy hand,
And mercy was the consort of thy power.
Victor, but humble, thou didst return, and in that
hour
To bury all dead sorrow was thy sole command,
And to live happy in our native land,

Remembering not that slaughter far away.
Thy voice in my heart calls out to me to avenge
thy death.
> [*Suddenly a second shepherd rushes down the
> mountain, plunges through the eddying
> crowd, and cries out to* POLLUX.

THE SECOND SHEPHERD.
Oh this new crime at which night holds its breath!
Electra, following your brother in his course,
While he had stooped to drink at the hollow of a
source,
With a sure stroke struck him, and slew him.

POLLUX.   She
Avenges us all. Swiftly she understood
That I could not plunge my hands in my own
brother's blood;
She understood, I tell you, and dealt the blow for me.
> [*About to go to* HELEN.
And my sister knows not yet, and in her house she
weeps and moans.

SCENE IV

Nobles, the Crowd, POLLUX

A NOBLE.
Sparta laments, struck with dismay.
Our smiling lasted scarce a day.

THE SECOND SHEPHERD. [*Continuing his tale.*]
Castor was fleeing, with feet in the rustling cones,
From turning to turning;
Water tempted him;

300

HELEN OF SPARTA

His lips with fever were burning;
He bent down; knelt on one knee,
By a spring's rim.
Then suddenly
The knife plunged into his back, to the hilt,
And the water he had scooped in his hand was spilt.
One arm's sweep has ended his devious ways;
His body stirs not in the long grass it has bent;
While over him, of a sudden indifferent,
The strange eyes of Electra gaze.

A NOBLE.
The gods put in her heart this zeal,
And thrust into her hands the avenging steel.

THE SECOND SHEPHERD.
Her face was untroubled, smooth in every line;
Her calmness was to us a terrible sign.   [*Pause.*
Then two woodmen, coming home from the wood,
Raised the body streaming with blood,
And carried it to their cottage among the pines;
While the shepherds carried Menelaus home through
      the vines.

A NOBLE.
The King had nearly run his course;
But Castor, whom the plains of Eurotas fed
With valour, and with warlike force!

SIMONIDES.
And now that Menelaus is dead,
Now that Pyrrhus is Hermione's thrall, now that
      Orestes has fled,
What king shall Lacedemonia obey?
                                        [*Numerous cries.*
Pollux, Pollux, Pollux! Let us place the crown on
      his head!

HELEN OF SPARTA

SIMONIDES. [*Continuing.*]
I recognize that as long as he wielded sway
Sparta proclaimed him faithful, wise, and just,
And that when his reign was over he yielded his
      trust
Without revolt to the former King, as in duty bound,
When home from Asia he came, with victory
      crowned.
I know he honours the gods, as a good king must,
And that he is supple in counsel and deserves the
      crown,
But Castor is his brother and struck Menelaus down.

A SHEPHERD.
All men here hold Pollux to be good.

SIMONIDES.
What matters? In his veins is the assassin's blood,
And interest ever is crime's reason.
Can we be sure his plans harboured no treason?
Was Castor his dupe or his accomplice?

ALL THE SHEPHERDS.   Lies!
Slanderer! Rascal! Traitor! Blind are your eyes!

SIMONIDES.
Be ye not angry! Not with malice do I speak,
But prudently. And nothing for myself I seek.

A SHEPHERD.
In us you hate and envy those whom Pollux protects.

A VINEDRESSER.
You would revive the quarrels of the towns and
      sects.

ANOTHER.
Pitfalls and traps are hidden in your words,
And in your bitterness resentment girds.

HELEN OF SPARTA

A NOBLE. [*Friendly to the shepherds. To* SIMONIDES.]
Your ardour only awakens sleeping hate, and casts
    a slur
On Pollux who, the while we wrangle, is away
With Helen in her house of grief, consoling her.

EUPHORAS.
Though I should in my turn offend, I say,
Since Helen has been here, murder is rife,
And prowls among us with his reeking knife.

[*From all sides.*] Impious mouth! O impious mouth!

EUPHORAS. [*Continuing.*]   I say that naught,
Not even to see her mourning her husband, frees
    me from the thought,
Now she is with us, of what evil may befall.

A SHEPHERD.
Let him who speaks in this wise be cast out by all!
Yea, let him with wife and child
To regions where no light is be exiled.

A YOUNG MAN.
For her, they fought more than ten years at Troy;
And never a man renounced the pride and joy
Of challenging death, which is life's thief.

EUPHORAS.
No beauty is worth a country's grief.

ALL.
Cowardice! Cowardice!

EUPHORAS.   Beware the race whose bloom
Is Helen, and whose hole Tyndareus is,
With Pollux and Castor for its savage boughs.

HELEN OF SPARTA

A Shepherd.
Never the son of Zeus has suffered such a gibe as
   this!

Simonides. [*Supporting* Euphoras.]
Euphoras is right; his keen eyes pierce
A thousand plans hidden from you that drowse.

A Shepherd.
Better than he do we see, and in numbers we are
   more,
And we are the city!

Simonides.   You are the arms of it!

A Shepherd. [*Shaking his fist at* Simonides.]
May your slanderous tongue be withered and split!

A Young Man. [*Also shaking his fist.*]
May the lightning burn your house to the floor!

Another. [*Following suit.*]
Let none of us, henceforth, come near you!
       [*Great tumult. Enter* Pollux *from the
          Palace; he steps on to the terrace. Some
          of the crowd rush towards him.*

A Shepherd. [*Pointing to* Pollux, *and crying to all.*]
Here Pollux comes, who shall be our lord and king!

Pollux [*After a long pause; he addresses himself
      particularly to those who are hostile to him; these
      are grouped to the* L. *of the stage.*
I have heard the rumble of your wretched quarrelling,
And was in fear lest my sister too should hear you:
She is alone now, weeping for her spouse
Far from all noise, at the heart of her great house.

HELEN OF SPARTA

If more than my high glory I did not esteem
Sparta's welfare, and your pride of being above all
They of whom it is said: " They are most rich, and
    mighty withal,
And zealous that their fruits and herds shall teem,"
I had not raised my voice but let your cries go by.
But you, whose discourse unto chiding tends,
Tell me what man has used his life to better ends
For Sparta's glory, and for her sons, than I?
I taught you, I, how vines are pruned to yield
The great, good grapes; and if you cleared the field
Where lemons thrive along Eurotas' far-famed
    shores,
I helped you with my counsel and my wealth.
Like a tamed horse the soil obeys you. At your
    doors
The water wells that brings your household health;
Fortune flows unto you, a tributary tide;
And Sparta, once a village, is a city now.
What matters it if you are thankless? Mine is the
    pride
Of having served you, and of remembering how,
That I to serve you again may be more keen,
Even you, whose hatred at this moment is turning
Round my calm forehead and my eyes serene.

SIMONIDES.
None hates you.

A SHEPHERD. [*To the noble.*]
          Why then was the bitter, burning
Reproach bandied about from man to man?

A SHEPHERD. [*To the other shepherd.*]
Let Pollux speak! He appeases and convinces.

EUPHORAS.
Let him defend himself!

HELEN OF SPARTA

POLLUX.   Alas! If with my little skill I can . . .
But if among us here Nestor, most agèd of princes,
Were present, his clear mind and moving tongue
Would tell you what man I was when I was young,
In the golden days when with him to Colchis I
    sailed.
He instructed my youth; and on the ship Argo then
Nestor through long months taught me the riddles
    of fate.
Supple wisdom I learned from the wisest of men,
And his zeal without respite, and his strength with-
    out hate.
I can show a people where the roads to fortune lie;
Helen's brother and the son of Zeus am I,
And Castor never had our blood in his veins.

EUPHORAS.
Castor is dead, Helen is the danger that remains.

POLLUX.
Speak not so, and rather say
That but for her, glory and its fiery wings
Had never touched the forehead of Greece and its
    kings.
Races that are strong need anguish, and if they
Would grow yet greater by danger they must be
    tried.   [Pause.
Friends, do you remember that at Troy, where the
    gates stood,
When evening fell across the ravaged countryside,
And when Helen was walking, alone, in the dying
    light,
Those who saw her passing, from the towers' height,
Would say: "What to us are death and war and
    blood,

And the fall on the heavy earth of bodies gashed
    and torn,
And the din of clashing chariots and of arms,
Since there was never yet a woman born
Fairer than her who fills our hearts with these
    alarms?"
Thus they reasoned, and they were vanquished men!
And, without hearing their praise, my sister passed
    by them then,
And you, the victors, dare to heap her name with
    calumny.
            [All protests are hushed. POLLUX *continues.*
But I will forget your rash, strange words, and see
Only the stirrings in your hearts of a passing fit.
                    [All acclaim him.
Higher from this trial Sparta must rise again,
And from the grief in which the King's death
    plunges it.
More sacred still is Helen in her widowhood,
And now that of her kin I am the last.
Of all men murder has stricken the most good,
But when his honoured corse to the pyre has
    passed
Say to yourselves that my sister and I
Are all that of Menelaus remains to-day. *[A pause.*
And now, I know that but one word had reconciled
Your hearts and mine, and made them beat as one,
    as in days gone by.
I tell you then—for I see the secret must be
    confessed—
That Zeus, my father, fixed my fate when I was a
    child.
I can hear his voice still speaking in my breast:
It is not **I**, but he who pronounces: "Master thou
    shalt be,
And conquered nations shall submit to thee."

HELEN OF SPARTA

Fain from the heavy diadem had I freed my brow,
But Zeus is all-powerful and to his will I bow;
And since in my own despite I obey the skies,
Proclaiming myself King, do you obey likewise.
                                    [*Acclamations.*

CURTAIN

ACT IV

Scene I

Helen. [*On the bench on which she sat in Act I.*]
M Y tears, the last,
      To thee I give,
O Menelaus, consort and king,
Whom jealous earth close covers and. holds fast.
O Menelaus, consort and king,
I shed my lonely grief above
Thy death, and what remains of our dark love.
My heart was worn with the roads of the earth;
      my doom
It was to wander with a barren womb.
But thou, ever forgetful and forgiving,
Didst take me back after my sinful living.
My tears, the last,
To thee I give!
Tranquil days under thy roof I would have passed,
In the smooth silence of monotonous hours;
I would have bent over thy winter my autumn
      flowers,
And simply, I would have loved to submit to thy
      yoke.
O Menelaus, consort and king,
I am here, lonely and poor, at the threshold of thy
      dwelling,
Where yestere'en for the last time thy heart spoke.
See my eyes that are humble; see the tears in my
      beautiful eyes up-welling;

HELEN OF SPARTA

Hearken to the last sound my voice shall make.
Soon my voice will be silent, with my heart's long
    ache.
O Menelaus, consort and king,
Before I join thee in the night whither thou hast
    past,
Take, oh take
My tears, the last!

Scene II

Pollux *and* Helen

POLLUX.
Victory and joy, my sister, to you I bring;
Your mourning shall be burnt up in my glory's fire;
Not for a day shall you cease to be Queen, for the
    people desire,
Being guided, and vouchsafing to each new king,
Whom fate sends, their confidence and fervent love,
To keep you on the throne, and to set me there at
    your right hand.
Queen you remain, and I am made King of the land.
Our country, which our parents raised above
The lands of the earth, declares for its divine
Children, and if the gods decree that you and I
Should burn superbly like two stars in the sky,
Let us prepare, ruling the proud earth, to reign
Empurpled in a glory that shall never wane.

HELEN.
O Menelaus, forgotten already is thy name!

HELEN OF SPARTA

POLLUX.
Come, let the dead sleep. Here life stands with its
    dower
Of beauty, life full of impatient flame;
To you it has been rebellious, harsh until this hour,
But I will tame and make magnificent your fate.

HELEN.
Too late, too late!

POLLUX.   No, it is never too late.
Fortune rises and follows my chariot, which shall
    race
O'er the multitudinous roads of shuddering space:
My vaguest wishes are made flesh, and breed
Corporeal substances of tangible lines.
I come, I am listened to, and all my designs,
Veiled or unveiled, unfailingly succeed;
Fury and hate I soothe; I banish all distress;
And if I but move my hand I fashion happiness.

HELEN.
Oh madness of men!

POLLUX.   Oh veritable power!
Pride is the wheat; despair the tares;
In Sparta in the agora the nation stands,
With conquered eyes, beating hearts, and lifted
    hands,
Casting their cries up to you, their vows, and their
    prayers;
Fathers and sons, daughters and mothers, all of them
    came;
They sent me to you, and the ardour I bring is
    theirs.

HELEN OF SPARTA

Come and hear the love that pants in their voices,
Come and rejoice in the fervour of a nation that
    rejoices;
It is I whom they call upon, but you they acclaim.

HELEN.
Why should I know again what I have known too
    long?

POLLUX.
All the earth exults and kisses your bare feet
With the burning mouth of its crowds surging
    along;
Cast down your pain which rebels; come out into
    life which is sweet.
Be born again; the hour is rare, and in my heart I
    feel
Such certain strength, such power victorious,
That there is nothing in the world I fear for either
    of us.
I am King; I reign; and fate I hold in a hand of
    steel.

HELEN.
What matters it to me whether you reign or no,
In this sad land accursed to coming times.
If all its torrents and great waters should overflow,
They could not ever wash away its crimes.
My will is dead, and has no goal;
Your boasting makes me hate even what is good;
All my being is broken to the deeps of my soul.
Now there is not a spark of pride in my blood,
No fire in my wasted breast, no light in my eyes.

POLLUX.
You merit the misfortunes that your spirit blight.

HELEN OF SPARTA

When yesterday you implored me with a spirit set
    on fire
By the mad assault of infamous desire,
In spite of your grief, erect in you I descried
Firmness, ardour, revolt, and pride,
And I promised you my willing aid; to-day,
Suddenly, without reason, your strength gives way;
The brotherly support I offered you you flout;
You go as though you were blind to meet the night;
Not a cry of pride in your breast rings out;
You care not though your beauty should be ruined
    in men's sight;
And all this happens, and all these things are said,
Because a man you never loved is dead.

HELEN.
Love him! I did more, I vowed my life to him.
A zeal, a tenderness intimate, unsated,
Which until then I had never found in the dim
Folds of my heart by the world immolated,
Renewed my being to its very core.
The King was happy if he but saw me, and still
    more
To feel me sitting near him at the day's declining.
I was the peaceable fire in the night shining;
And he knew me faithful, and tender in every caress,
For my hand was calm with a mother's gentleness.

POLLUX.
Farewell! You are overcome, and no longer will I
    seek
To raise to my height your brow irresolute and
    weak;
You are Helen no more; to the world you are a
    stranger;
And your uncertain fortune with one stroke I part

From mine, which is too beautiful, and is in danger,
Dallying here, of changing like your ruined heart.
Those who come too near it, misfortune chokes;
The wind of the tempest tatters purple cloaks:
I fear your presence. Farewell! Farewell!

HELEN.   Go!

SCENE III

ELECTRA *and* HELEN

ELECTRA *enters with slow, wearied steps.*

HELEN.   You!

ELECTRA.
I have wandered since last night in the pale gloom,
O'er narrow forest paths alone, without rest;
Now I discover no longer in my breast
That black, wild heart of mine that clamoured for
        the tomb;
The hatred in my blood, I feel, is sinking now;
A last few hours of peace are granted to my brow.

HELEN.
You have avenged my husband by striking my
        brother down.
But you, alas! did only slay the one to gloat above
Your victim, and in his streaming blood to drown
The jealous fury of your guilty love.
And in one person thus you are justice and crime,
As your kindred were at Mycenæ, in olden time.

HELEN OF SPARTA

ELECTRA.
It is Menelaus, Menelaus alone that your eyes
    mourn,
He alone who was tender to you and forgiving,
    while,
In his own home, of lustful desires you were the
    bourne,
While in the shadow his death was plotted with
    venomous guile.
O King! The assassin struck you when I was by,
Struck you before my eyes under the forest trees,
Before my eyes who am myself an Atrides and your
    niece.
Into my dolorous arms you sank without a cry,
With your sad mouth closed, and straightway you
    were dead.
The thought of you sustained my steps when after
    Castor I ran,
When sudden vengeance with madness filled my
    head,
And you armed my hand with courage, O great old
    man!
O heart of goodness, peace, and wisdom made,
Assassinated from a coward's lurking-place,
Whose ruthless hand by your weakness was not
    stayed.   [*Point-blank to* HELEN.
What would you have done?

HELEN.   Alas!

ELECTRA.   His blood
Splashed over my hand that sought to close his
    wound.
I gazed in his eyes that heard my voice as he
    swooned
Making my moan to the gods in the green wood.

HELEN OF SPARTA

Why were you not there with us, Helen, in the
  forest's dark?
Why could you not hear, where you were, my
  savage cry,
Before in death the lines of his face had grown stark?
I felt his body growing cold;
And fain had I given my life and my soul to hold
His days back that were fleeting fast to death,
But alas! I had only my poor woman's breath
Which could not warm, alas! his mangled frame!

HELEN.
Oh burning vengeance! Oh harrowing grief and
  shame!

ELECTRA.
My breast breathes lighter since my hand was moved
  to strike,
And calmness with the gloam has fallen, like
A deep repose, on my bewilderment.
The keen eyes of the swarming stars have swept
My upturned face, and I have felt no dread;
I have thought of my mad race with blood besprent,
And, tired with happiness, long have I wept.
Assassins, crimes, and victims crowd the course of
  time,
And all this blood upon the roadways shed!
And the oldest murder and the latest crime
Seemed, but just now, united in my hand;
And my halting reason and dark mind were forced
  to turn
Round all this horror and could not understand;
And ever my long tears, as though escaping from
  an urn,
Flowed from my eyes and ne'er could dry.
> [*She has sat down, and* HELEN *has sat
> down near her.*

HELEN OF SPARTA

HELEN. Alas! I too
Am troubled in spirit and know not what to do;
All your ills I also have known, and your heart's
 burn;
And yet, I sit here at your side,
And in your tears there is some charm that stills
 our strife.
Oh these evils that roll us in their ebb and tide!
Oh the air of these black times with poison rife!
Oh all this blood shed under your virgin's eyes,
So that your poor hands also might grow used to it!
We come from so far away, where the dense dark-
 ness lies,
Unto this end, and now we are mingling, where
 we sit,
Our gloomy thoughts, our misery, and our cries,
And we dare not say yet we forgive each other.
I knew you a child at the house of my sister, your
 mother;
Your sad eyes shone under your great pale brow.
One night, you were weeping your dead dreams, as
 you do now,
They brought you to me to sleep with me in my
 bed;
I took your hands and caressed your hair,
And you fell asleep listening to what I said,
Like a summer fruit rocked on the shady bough.
 [*For some minutes,* HELEN *has unconsciously
 been caressing* ELECTRA's *hair.*

ELECTRA.
O Helen! Spare me! Oh take care, take care!
You are awakening the fury in my heart afresh!
Oh your hands on my brow! Oh your hands on my
 hair!
Oh your sudden breath on your foe-woman's flesh,

317

HELEN OF SPARTA

And your fingers, and your arms, and your body,
  and your eyes!

HELEN. [*Who has risen.*]
Oh the leaps of your heart through your misery!

ELECTRA. [*Bewildered.*]
Helen! Helen!

HELEN. [*Recovering possession of herself.*]
                Leave me! Go away from me!
Not for a moment may I taste of peace.
We are both ripe for death, unfit to live.

ELECTRA.
Helen!

HELEN. Alas! I was forgetting, and being kind!
But nothing is granted me, not even to forgive!
All human ills within me ring without surcease,
Cruelly clashing, and struggling for my heart.
Oh my dolorous fate! Oh my frantic mind!
In silence, and with no weeping, let us part,
And, following both our destiny, let us haste
To die, no matter where, deep in the night.

HELEN OF SPARTA

HELEN, ZEUS, *two Shepherds*

HELEN *ascends the terrace.* ELECTRA, *not daring to follow her, wanders for some time in silence round the Palace, and in the end disappears.*

HELEN.
O night, calm empire of Diana the chaste,
Come set thy silvery feet on the grass chill with
    dew;
Night of funereal and pale and glacial cold,
Who to the seas and the vast skies dost lend thine
    azure hue;
Night of white silence and of a darkness of gold;
Night of the roving gods from star to star that pass
To fix their fate or hurl them through the vasts of
    space,
Mingle my sorrow with their ruin and their death!
                    [*Two shepherds have glided on to the stage
                        in the foreground, and now they talk
                        and point to the forest, without at first
                        seeing* HELEN.

FIRST SHEPHERD.
I tell you that numberless eyes the sylvan shadow
    gem,
And the pines are astir as though they had life and
    breath!
If you have never seen satyrs, you can see them
    now . . . if you dare!

319

HELEN OF SPARTA

SECOND SHEPHERD.
I am afraid.

FIRST SHEPHERD.
        Fear nothing: I am known to them.
With the milk of my goats I make them fat. Look
    there! . . .
There is one of them leaning where the dewy
    branches glisten;
All the forest is stirring and singing: listen, listen . . .
                [Noises in the foliage.

SECOND SHEPHERD.
It is the jolting of a cart, somewhere, on the high-
    way.

FIRST SHEPHERD.
I tell you, their mad voices are sounding by forest
    and fell,
And if we listen closely we can tell
What the tangled woods to the smooth meadows
    say.

A SATYR.
Thou who art come from Asia, O Helen, with thy
    beauty undimmed,
Heavy with suffered love and prisoned sighs,
It is we, it is we, the gliding satyrs shaggy-limbed,
Who call thee to us to-night in our raving cries;
The earth is soft and warm, and the caves are deep
    in leaves . . .
Everything fades in the shadow, and nature never
    grieves;
And among us thy heart will remember not.

HELEN OF SPARTA

SECOND SHEPHERD.
Oh miracle!

FIRST SHEPHERD.
      Be silent!
      [HELEN *leans forward in the direction*
              whence the noise comes.

A SATYR.   We are frenzied lusts,
And the clasp of the wind when at the red wood he
    thrusts;
Hairy our flesh is; and desire immense and hot
Dances, writhes, and beats the earth in our mad feet;
The grass, the soil, the mountain, and the deep
    valleys,
And the sudden gleams piercing like holes the dark
    woodland alleys,
All this is ourselves when we love in the earth's lap;
And our lascivious, bestial sweat is the world's sap.

HELEN.
Ye gods!

FIRST SHEPHERD.
      Well then?

SECOND SHEPHERD.   Confusedly I hear,
But do not understand.

FIRST SHEPHERD.
          They are crying to Helen, it is clear.
The leaves are stirring all along the plain,
And the air, heavy with odours, is all a-shiver.
Look down there at the glistening of the river:
The Naiads are going to speak. Listen again. . . .

HELEN OF SPARTA

A NAIAD.
Helen, O thou that livest, breathing among earth's
    daughters,
In a body brighter than the starry firmament,
Our grottoes of light and our translucent waters
With glittering gems shall make thee a moving tent.
In our liquid arms love is supple, and sweet, and
    fresh,
And long, long kisses of gold shall glide o'er thy
    flesh.

HELEN.
Oh never again to hear, or touch, or see!
O ye gods! what have I done to the river and the
    wood
That the sinuous water suddenly should flood
My heart with anguish and lift its winding arms to
    me?

FIRST SHEPHERD. [*Arrived, with his companion, at
the background.*]
Look up there where the stadium bends round. . . .
    See:
Bacchantes mad on the hills are those fires that
    shine;
Listen, listen again.

A BACCHANTE.   The Thyades are we,
And our bodies are aflame, Helen, with love of thee;
The darkness makes us drunk, and burns us like
    black wine,
And our dancing by night to its roots the forest
    shocks.
We hear in the gloaming the whispering of the
    rocks

HELEN OF SPARTA

Telling us, when they see thee passing, their secret
    dream;   ·
And the rocks and the soil, and the very thickets feel
Strange shudders running through them when thy
    coming awakes
Their sleep, and the very pebble loves thee, shivers
    and shakes,
When in thy passing thou touchest it with thy
    naked heel.

HELEN.
O to perish utterly and pass away!
Where shall I walk henceforth, where shall I sleep,
Where shall I breathe without suffering by night or
    day?
What is there round me that will not arise and
    make my flesh start and creep?
Depart from me, fresh lips of the water, breath of
    the breeze,
Scent of the flowers, leaves of the moving trees,
Dawns, noons, and eves, and even you, O light!

A SATYR.
Helen!

HELEN. And you,
Shadow of mountains, and you, wind that grasps
    and groans,
And you, sharp eyes that glitter in stones.

NAIADS.
Helen! Helen!

HELEN.   Oh misery of my body, ever new!
Oh tears of my eyes in the vain dust! All that is
Holds me and drives me mad with kiss on kiss!

HELEN OF SPARTA

A BACCHANTE.
Helen! Helen! Helen!

HELEN.　　　　　For me there is no resting-place!
Will not the earth in my grave be the last of my
　　　lovers,
And, as my cold and docile frame it covers,
Kindle my flesh close clasped in its embrace?
O Zeus, force of the world, king of the subtle air,
Here are my arms stretched up to thee, here is my
　　　prayer:
The deep earth fills me with horror and affright,
I feel that even there love with its fire and pain
　　　may lie;
And since no refuge remains to me by day or night,
In the gaping ground, under the open sky,
Annihilate me utterly, thou judge of monarch and
　　　slave!
Death I refuse, annihilation I crave.

> *[A great light shines out, and falls across
> the front of the stage. The two shep-
> herds, who have come back to the middle
> of the stage, see* ZEUS *above them, and
> raise their arms to him.*

ZEUS. [*Invisible.*]
Hearken, thou who to men wert Helen, I have
　　　heard thy cries,
Here I unveil myself, Zeus, Lord of the Skies;
Nor pain nor grief thy poor heart overcame,
Though love it knew, which puts the gods to shame.
Lo! The black void thy frantic prayer desires
Exists not under the heaven's revolving fires;
All things are wed and are shed, and parted are
　　　every pair,
But only to mingle again in an infinite life elsewhere.

HELEN OF SPARTA

Terror, and sobs, and cries over the earth's face
    sweep
But as the morning mists cover the mountain's steep;
The immutable mystery they never shock,
Which is the real life of the deep, hard rock.
Thou shouldst have seized the ills that mocked thy
    dream,
To twist their strength and fire to thy will supreme.
But thou wert a woman: beauty was thy law;
Thy brow was not remote in pride and awe.
Die; but be born again; to suffer, if needs must be!
Thy old fate yields to thy new destiny:
Here are my lightning and my thunders, to bear
    thee on high
To my love of god and of a father, in the sky.
      [*Thunder-clap.* HELEN *is lifted up into the sky.*

CURTAIN

325